The American Rhythm

The American Rhythm

Studies and Reëxpressions of Amerindian Songs

BY

MARY AUSTIN

New and Enlarged Edition

New York
COOPER SQUARE PUBLISHERS, INC.
1970

DEDICATED

TO

WILLIAM ARCHER

BY WHOSE INTEREST IN THESE STUDIES
I WAS FIRST CONFIRMED IN THEIR SIGNIFICANCE
TO AMERICAN LITERATURE.

ACKNOWLEDGMENTS

For permission to reprint the above poems I am indebted to the following magazines: *Harper's Weekly, The Bookman, McClure's, Everybody's, Poetry, The Dial, The Forum, The Double Dealer, Harper's, The Quill.* "The Much Desired" is from *Christ in Italy;* "Woman," from *Love and the Soul Maker;* "The Song of the Mateless Woman" from the original verses of *The Arrow Maker.*

CONTENTS

MAGIC FORMULAS

TRIBAL LAYS

The American Rhythm

The American Rhythm

I

§ 1

In this connection we begin at once to think of rhythm as experience.

MacDougall [1] calls it "an immediate affection of the consciousness, depending on a particular kind of sensory experience." But this affection of consciousness, the passing of the perception of rhythmic forms arising fortuitously in our environment—as the roll of thunder or the run of wind in tall grass—through the sensorium into the subconscious, is experiential in its nature. It leaves a track, a mold, by which our every mode of expression is shaped. What we have here to do with, is the activity of an organism, the experience of rhythm as distinct from our intellectual perception of it.

Rhythmic forms are constantly presenting themselves to our perceptional experience, but before they can be reckoned with they must initiate the factor of movement. Such movement arises subconsciously in us in response to recurrent series of homogeneous stimuli. But the mere intellectual appreciation of such sequences is not

[1] For this and succeeding references, see Appendix.

3

enough. There must be a series of motor impulses started somewhere, before the experience is appreciated as rhythmic, and MacDougall [2] goes so far as to suggest that if the motor responses which we habitually make to rhythmic stimuli, the tappings of finger and foot, the nodding of the head, are inhibited, there will be a lessened perception of rhythm.

The suggestibility of the human organism in the direction of rhythmic response is so generous that the rhythmic forms to which the environment gives rise, seem to pass through the autonomic system, into and out of the subconscious without our having once become intellectually aware of them. Rhythm, then, in so far as it affects our poetic mode, has nothing to do with our intellectual life. It is located in the dimension of appreciable stress. Its measure is the measure of the capacity of opposing organic strains.

The only indispensable condition for the acquirement of new rhythms and their use, is that the points of stress recurrence should lie within the normal stress capacity of the organism. The recurrence must not be so rapid as to disrupt the organism nor prolonged beyond the capacity of the organism to remain in the process of movement without coming to rest. That is to say, rhythm to be enjoyed and deliberately reproduced must lie within the limits of pleasurable exercise.

But we need not conclude that the succession of muscular tensions and releases, of which we are all aware in the enjoyment of rhythm, are necessarily set in motion by sensory stimuli, sight, sound, or touch.

The major rhythms of the human organism are given

by the blood and the breath. What is the familiar trochee but the *lub*-dub, *lub*-dub of the heart, what the hurrying of the syllable in the iambus but the inhibition of the blood by the smaller vessels? Within the organism many minor organs have each their distinctive rhythmic tempo, both nervous and functional. Very probably rhythm is a factor in thought formation. There are at any rate recognizable alternations of attack and relaxation of the cognitive process.

If we think of consciousness as Philosophy gives us increasing leave to do, as energetic in its nature, we have a concept of wave-like motion as the normal procedure, possibly the very mode of being itself. Moreover, the chemical changes which, as we now understand, mark the successive stages by which the emotions take possession of the organism, have each their own recognizable rhythmic modes. Thus we represent, each one of us, an orchestration of rhythms which, subjectively coordinated, produce the condition known as well-being.

Since the very existence of the organism is dependent on such successful coördination, the adaptive capacity of each distinctive rhythm must be great. Let any one of them attain a position of dominant stress, and the whole organism is brought into subjective obedience to it, or ruptures itself in the attempt. So one dies of love or anger, or makes poetry of them, according to the measure of personal subjectivity.

Every ordinarily introspective individual is aware of these rhythmic adjustments going on in himself, varying with the character of the stimuli. Given a suitable arrangement of the stimuli, as in orchestrated music or poetic drama properly recited, or the consciousness of reciprocated passion, and the whole energetic plane of the organism is raised.[3]

Here we have a basis for the poetic quest, and for the establishment of a traditional poetic mode, provocative of the maximum of well-being. The rhythms which give pleasure are those into which the organism has naturally fallen in the satisfaction of the social urge, the ego urge, the mating urge. Where the path to such satisfactions is deeply graven, the poet falling into it will find the whole sum of sensory material enriched by association. Where by changed motor habits the initial association is obliterated, and only the swing remains, the old rhythm will arise, at the recurrence of a given stimulus, with sourceless connotations of authority to which we give the name of instinct when we observe them in others, and inspiration in ourselves.

Meumann, Stumpf, MacDougall, Dalcroze,[4] many sincere investigators, give us leave to think of rhythm as inherited. Even the mechanists admit the passing with the germ plasm of potentialities for all the organic rhythms on which anything that we can reasonably call a rhythmic sense is founded. All we require then, for the inheritability of rhythms developing in response to stimuli appearing late in the history of the generations, is an admission that the incremental realizations called forth by experiences peculiar to that generation, shall become a determining factor in the potentiality of the succeeding generation. If this is admitted it makes very little difference whether you treat the increment of potentiality as inheritance or as instinct. For what is instinct in this connection but the memory of motor-emotional experience reduplicated often enough to set up a habit of response, the habit persisting after the memory of the associated fatigues have faded? Or, if you prefer to place our appetite for repetitive sequences of such experiences in the domain of a "rhythmic sense" which, functioning automatically, achieves a subjective binding into a whole of sequential stimuli, we have still, before we can use any given sequence as a poetic medium, to push back the initial experience beyond our memory of its associated fatigues. An instinctive rhythm is a habit of response of which the initiative is lost. Being lost is one of the conditions of our making poetry of it. Much of the pleasure of versification is in the discovery in ourselves of inestimable treasures of swinging thought, swinging with a momentum that exceeds the expenditure of consciousness as the swing of a skipping rope exceeds the effort of the wrist that turns it. And how could those initial fatigues be more surely lost than in the passage of the habit of response from the parent to the offspring?

Imitation plays its part, but what better evidence could there be of the failure of the imitated gesture to evoke a high type of poetic realization than the kind of verse that has been evoked in America in those temples of Imitation, the Universities?

Nor, though almost every poet has tried it, can true poetic affectiveness be secured by the verbally imitative reproduction, however skilful, of sequential stimuli occurring in nature. True evocation is from the autonomic centers of *experience*.

The physical basis of poetry appears, then, as the orchestration of organic rhythms under the influence of associated motor and emotional impulses, recapitulated from generation to generation. Of these influences two are outstanding and of measurable variability: the motor habit by which man wrests his living from the earth, and the social habit by which he relates himself to his kind. What experience is older or comes closer to the life of man than his Two-handedness? Taker and Holder: the play of them, one into the other; strike with the right, cover with the left; thus he conceived his Universe, two-handed.

To this day, according as our racial ancestor tucked his weapon under one arm to count out his kill on the fingers of that hand, do we write, up and down, from right to left, or left to right, as the nature of the weapon dictated the hand to be held. And are not Taker and Holder the protagonists of the first drama, even as the Amerind conceived them, Ahayuta, Matsalema, the eternal Twin Brethren, right and left hands of Sun Power? One of them pulls the life-force up through the dust to corn, and the other pulls the corn back to dust. In this fashion, at least, primitive song measure is beaten out—right, left—right, left . . . and in time, as use made them not quite two paired, but two compensating organs, left, left, *right!*

So is all art form shaped on a system of oppositions, balance without parity. What we mean by composition in art is simply right and left handedness, one hand and a pot hook. To a three-handed race all our pictures would lack balance, all our rhythms leave the sense suspended.

Thus if we go back far enough into the origin of simple poetic rhythms, we find the gesture by which in the Days-of-the-New the earth was conquered. If we look for the resolution of intricacies of rhythm called classic, we find it in the dance, and if we go back in the history of the dance we find the pattern by which men and women, friends and foes, welded themselves into societies and became reconciled to the Allness. Here we find economy of stress giving rise to preferred accents, and social ritual establishing the tradition of sequence.

Given a new earth to live on, new attacks on the mastery of time and space, and a whole new scale of motor impulses is built into the subconscious structure of the individual. Given a new experiential adaptation of social mechanisms, and all the emotive and cognitive processes set themselves to its tune. Given, as happened in the United States, an emotional kick *away* from the old habits of work and society, and a new rhythmic basis of poetic expression is not only to be looked for, but is to be welcomed. It becomes evidence of the extent to which the American experience has "taken," among the widely varying racial strains that make up its people.

§ 2

Almost anybody might have predicted the rise of a new verse form in America. This was implicit in the necessity of restating the national consciousness in terms of the burgeoning American outlook; and without any knowledge of the rhythms in which the land had already expressed itself, two or three things might have confidently been prophesied about it.

It would be a form as lacking in tradition as the American experiment itself. It would be democratic in the sense that it would be within the capacity of the democratically bred. Anybody could use it, as anybody always has been able to use native verse form freely. Finally, it would be a statement of life as for the first two or three hundred years, life presented itself on the western continent, in terms of things lived through rather than observed or studied.

English speaking verse forms, as they were used by the English classicists at the beginning of the American era, were largely derived. Greek, which was foot music, movement of communal labor at the wine press and around the altar in the market place; Roman, which to the Greek dance added the lyric intricacy of personal passion; and Hebrew influences had gone to their making. In Hebrew verse, the influence of which on English form is never sufficiently taken into account, there is movement and rhythm of the sort that goes on inside a man's head, sitting on the housetop with his feet tucked under him; the perpetual balance of the soul between spirit and semblance; the setting one thing against another, ranging them in threes and fours, the search for authentic spiritual progressions.

To England and the English speaking, not one of these three was indigenous, and genetic only as the result of long selection. By this process they became the instrument of a selected class, the rhythms of privilege. For if the words folk-song, folk-dance, folk-music mean anything, they mean just this, that there are in that country superimposed forms of song and dance and music, marked off from the folk use by selective experiences of caste and class.

Periodically, energizations of the common thought through national experience displaced the brilliant, brittle crusts of classicism, and reshaped the prevailing literary modes. Thus in the times of Chaucer and of Shakespeare there was an emergence of the national spirit, and a fusion of the speech-streams which fed the Island tongue, energetic enough to overflow the classic molds and make new patterns of literary form, recognizably English.

When I speak of rhythm here, I am referring to the basic motor impulses which underlie the English gesture. These are of the simplest; the *lub*-dub, *lub*-dub of the heavy footed Nordics, lightened occasionally by the use of two shorts to balance the long movement. In this measure all their great poems of action are written; an exceedingly ancient measure beyond which there is but one more ancient, the pyrrhic, sounding so faintly at the far end of our Greek vista that many scholars have supposed it a purely theoretic measure of the Grammarians. But to the thousands of Americans who have listened to the swift patter of its unaccented dub dub, dub dub, dub dub, dub dub in the plazas of Zuñi and Oraibi it is the very pulse of emerging American consciousness.

This we shall come back to. The English, who are not a dancing people, did no better by themselves, unless you count the slight clipping of one of the shorts of their heroic measures and the equal lengthening of the other, a hint which I suspect they accepted from their horseback habits, as they made half a league, half a league onward. For all their moods of high sensibility, for the languors and raptures of beauty sensuously perceived, as well as to display the Gothic intricacy of their speech, they had recourse to the dance measures of the Classics, which by the era of American settlement had been transferred from the centers of self-realization and run off at the tips of waving swords or twinkling, lute-playing fingers.

Poetry· is a man's game. Women are only good at it by a special dispensation as men are occasionally good at millinery. If you look for the determinant of poetic form in a given period, look for the gesture by which maleness is in that age expressed. In Europe for a thousand years before American settlement began, the sword had been the extended flourish of man's personality, as the cloisteral pace was the measure of his profoundest meditation. In Elizabethan verse there was pomp, which folk never use, lute notes, which they could not if they would. America, though it carried too long like the dried shell of a locust, the shape of the derived culture of England on her back, proved no place for flourishes, nor this the time to go horsed on the poetic inventions of an earlier age.

It was back to the foot pace on the new earth, ax

stroke and paddle stroke. So it is that new rhythms are born of new motor impulses.

§ 3

The length of time required for a new set of motor habits to generate a habit of rhythmic response will depend somewhat on the native resiliency of the racial material worked upon. The process will be quickened or retarded by the intensity of the involved emotional complexes.

In the case of the settlement of the American colonies, these were of high intensity. Motivated by religious fervors or forced by political exigencies, they implied in almost every case, rending of old ties and facing of new terrors. Always the pull of the schools was toward the classic measures. But all the schools could do was counterbalanced by the influx of immigrant material which had never known the use of Greek and Roman forms. Whatever Russ and Pole and Serb had come to America for, it wasn't at least that they might learn to express themselves in pentamic hexameters. What they brought with them in the way of subconscious baggage had, in common with what they were to find in America, the similarities that all gestures of attack on the raw earth have to one another. In all folk expression the older layers of experience are at play. There was scope in the new America for play on the Homeric scale, but not to the tunes that, even in the form in which European scholarship first came by them, were already rhythms of privilege, the medium of a selected experience.

§ 4

Something also was added by the land. Poignancy is of the poet's soul, perhaps, but rhythm is always in his sense; eye and ear have each their part in it. Streams of rhythmic sights and sounds flowed in upon the becoming race of Americans from every natural feature. The great hegira from northern and central Europe had been largely motivated by the desire to escape from the over-humanized aspects of those lands. There was hunger in man for free flung mountain ridges, untrimmed forests, evidence of structure and growth. Life set itself to new processions of seed time and harvest, the skin newly tuned to seasonal variations, the very blood humming to new altitudes. The rhythm of walking always a recognizable background for our thoughts, altered from the militaristic stride to the jog of the wide, unrutted earth. Explorer, fur-trader, King's agent, whoever for three centuries followed it, must have carried a record of its foot work in his walk, a wider swing and recovery to his mind. As the pioneer track made westward-flowing patterns, the rhythm of horseback riding, of a rise and fall distinctively of the American continent, superseded the foot pace. Now and then one picks it up in the work of Vachel Lindsay and Carl Sandburg, and not only the saddle jog, but the unintermittent cluck and roll of the Overland Flyer.

Only a few months ago, when I had occasion to turn back to one of my desert books, written eighteen years ago and scarcely looked at since, I discovered the first paragraph striking without intention into the irregular tug and release of the four horse Mojave stage and of the eighteen-mule borax team, from which my association with the scenes described was almost never freed. Probably the deep self from which poetry springs picks up a new rhythm very quickly when there is little or no expenditure of physical energy, and the psyche is free to concern itself with wonder and delight.

We should have come into our heritage of rhythms based on the tug and heave of constructive labor much earlier, if all the time the common people were learning them, the intellectual caste had not been, in an environment artificially created for that purpose, sedulously putting the young through the ancient carpet-treading, croiser-bearing paces.

Emerson came stumbling into the American trail about Monadnoc. Lowell, brought up to think of poetry as a fountain spouting somewhere in the neighborhood of a university, found himself dipping up the vernacular to water the stale wine of his library. Longfellow, yearning after American material, fell short of realizing that the true form for it lay a little farther ahead, deeper in the wilderness, and turned back to Greece for the measures of *Evangeline*, to Finland for *Hiawatha*.

There was an American, however, whose nature had been so shaped to the wilderness track that his every public utterance, his homely anecdotes, even, were haunted by its rhythms. On one of these occasions when, as was reported in the newspapers of that day, "the President made a few remarks," he said:

> "The world will little note nor long remember
> What we say here:
> But it can never forget what they did here."

He was speaking of the dedication of a monument to a notable public service, but speaking from the innermost inner man, he fell unconsciously into the stride of one walking a woodland path with an ax on his shoulder. He spoke:

> "It is rather for us
> Here to be dedicated to the great task
> Remaining before us;
> That from these honored dead we take
> Renewed devotion to that cause
> For which they gave the last full measure of devotion.
> That we here highly resolve
> That these dead shall not have died in vain;
> That this nation under God
> Shall have a new birth of freedom."

Thus the rail splitter arrives at his goal with the upswing and the down-stroke:

> "That government of the people
> For the people
> By the people
> Shall not perish from the earth!"

And the ax comes to rest on the chopping log while a new length is measured.

It was natural that the new movement should show in oratory, always closer to the masses than any English verse had been since the Elizabethan period. Such a rhythm was to show itself in France after the fury of revolution, and in the emerging democracy of late Victorian times. Charles Dickens,[5] whenever he was moved—and it was the democratic spirit, the spirit of the fellowship of folk that moved him oftenest—fell into those measures that the French, always so much clearer about their processes, first called, though not the first to use them, *vers libre*. All such movements in Europe have one thing in common with the American movement: They represent the rhythm of men attempting to move concertedly from their own base, rather than to be waved forward and back by the batons of kings or academies.

Whitman's was the first clear and self-recognizing song of the road. Whitman was the type genius,—like Mark Twain, Stephen Crane, Theodore Dreiser and Carl Sandburg, to group them by type, without respect to the quality of their performance. He was sensitive to the bigness of things, which he mistook for universality, moved about a great deal, speculated freely, and was unclear in his conclusions; the American type. His whole personality swaggered with what more or less dominated the movement of the American procession, the consciousness of being entirely adequate to the environment. America was a woman, and the poet, though slightly befuddled by her effect upon him, had proved his manhood upon her.

But though he was sure, Americanly, that he was on his way, Whitman was by no means so deep in the wilderness as he supposed himself to be. He was seldom far from the rutted pioneer track, a place of chucks and wallows, dust choked in his time with the passing armies. Out of this dust, sweaty and raucous, we hear him chanting, principally of what he sees, so that his rhythms, more often than not, are mere unpatterned noises of the street.

". . . Bravuras of birds, bustle of growing wheat, gossip of flames, clack of two sticks cooking my meals.

". . . The flexible rise and fall of backs, the continual click
     of the trowels striking the bricks."

It was the genius of Whitman not so much to be a
poet as to be able to say out of what stuff the new
poetry was to be made. It was only when he occasionally turned aside into solitude that all the senses fused
themselves in the spirit's heat. Only thus does his verse
cease to be mere foot and eye record of his passage,
and exhibits the true brand of the American strain: goal
consciousness, and pattern attained by balance and a
system of compensating phrases.

Of this method it may be said that Whitman neither
discovered nor invented it; to the limit of his capacity
to respond he was used by it. His capacity was on every
side limited by his intelligence, which was adolescent and
gamboling. What one suspects of Whitman admirers to-
day is that the name is often invoked in justification of
what the poet and poetaster alike find going on in themselves—the urge and recovery of the democratic experience.

II

§ 5

All this time there was an American race singing in
tune with the beloved environment, to the measures of
life-sustaining gestures, taking the material of their songs
out of the common human occasions, out of the democratic experience and the profound desire of man to
assimilate himself to the Allness as it is displayed to

him in all the peacock splendor of the American continent. In so far as verse forms are shaped by topography and the rhythm of food supply, the aboriginal American was singing in precisely the forms that were later to become native to the region of Spoon River, the Land of Little Rain, and the country of the Cornhuskers. It was when I discovered that I could listen to aboriginal verses on the phonograph in unidentified Amerindian languages, and securely refer them by their dominant rhythms to the plains, the deserts and woodlands that had produced them, that I awoke to the relationships that must necessarily exist between aboriginal and later American forms. This was before 1900, before there was any movement more than was indicated by Whitman and the verse of Stephen Crane, which at that time I had not seen. Whitman I knew slightly, though I here confess that my interest in him swelled perceptibly in the discovery of how like the Indian's his method is, and how much less its emotional affectiveness.

I shall not, however, be able to put succinctly all that I have been able to observe of the evolution of tribal poetics until the psychologists [6] have provided me with a better concept of group-mindedness and popularized a terminology under which its various states can be handled. It appears, on the whole, that numbers of individual minds combine under variations of emotional stress very much as the dust grains on a sounding board are marshaled into patterns by the vibrations of the musical chord. That the Dawn Mind showed greater fluency, as well as greater intricacy of pattern response, seems indicated.

The development of pronominal words points to some sort of group-identity antedating the personal. Even yet there are tribes that have no word for "I" as distinguished from "ourselves." Also, among tribal groups we find communal song more highly developed than any form of personal expression. Among Amerindian tribes whose culture is for the most part of the type called neolithic we find a highly developed use of poetry both to express and to evoke states of mind which are in their nature social.

Even where tribal poetry seems to be most personal, it will often, on examination, be shown to be affective in character. The lover sings for the purpose of bringing the soul of the beloved into communion with his soul; the witch-doctor would bind the life of the victim with his charm; the medicine man, though he seems to be expressing himself in unrelated song sequences, is actually raising his own psychic states, plane by plane, to the pitch of communion with the Friend-of-the-Soul-of-Man by means of which cures are effected.

A man's Own Song, representing the highest pitch of coördination with his universe, reached through love, or meditation, or the triumph of his man-ness, is so peculiarly his possession that none may sing it without his permission. But it may be transferred as a legacy to the tribe, and so pass into the unrelated body of song lore, esteemed for qualities we have learned to call esthetic.

Thus the rhythm pattern may be preserved long after the words have become archaic, or have given place to newer statements of the idea presented. Where individual songs are found woven into the body of ritualistic dance-drama, it will be usually because some shreds of the first singer's luck in hunting, his prowess in war or his fortunate relation to the Allness is believed to inhere in the song. Thus are built up, much in the manner of the Roman Mass, those mimetic sequences of song, drama and recitative, requiring days sometimes for their completion, by which the psychic life of the tribe is co-ordinated. Among the Navaho there is a nine-day per-formance designed to make the smell of a man's own tribe seem a good smell to him, which is hopefully recom-mended to our young intellectuals.

That poetry may be of communal origin has long been the belief of scholars, but the lack of any adequate concept of the group-mindedness from which the poem may spring, has left the conviction rather hang-ing in the air. The nearest we have been able to ap-proach veridical group processes is in the making of ballads. Here we have dance movement, or a chanted burden, creating a plastic matrix within which the ballad takes shape by accretions of individual contribution, fitting into the common state created by the chant or dance movement so aptly as to insure acceptance by the group. This is probably a true description of the growth of certain of our European types of verse. But it must also be kept in mind that all our studies of European balladry are related to cultures much later than the neolithic.

Historically, Amerind culture appears to overlap the archaic Greek period which it precedes. What had hap-pened between the new Stone Age and the time in which ballad making was the social entertainment of unlettered peasantry, was that superior social castes had *usurped the people's rights to the use of poetry as a means of communication with the Allness*. The original communal use of poetry to energize the plane of socially defensive and offensive activities, had been taken over by the military caste. Prayer poetry, and poetic rites for the coördination of the group mind with Godhead came so strictly under the censorship of the priestly caste that the people not only no longer made their religious songs, but no longer understood them. But since no people can be long kept from poetizing, the common people of Europe fell back on the purely personal occasions, and on the deeds of heroes much nearer to them than the once celebrated gods. Thus the ballad, as we know it, becomes a recessive form, resorted to from secondary motives, and only occasionally rising, in the hands of some native genius, to the earlier levels of affectiveness.

In a later work I hope to deal with this passage of the communally affective uses of poetry out of the hands of the tribe into the control of restricted classes. For this work, which is a study of the rise of poetry among genuinely democratic groups, it will be enough to say that narrative poetry, and versified collections of tribal wisdom, which we do not find until near the end of the Neolithic culture, appear to be parasitic on the poetic impulse, due to the incidental discovery that in rhythmic form they are remembered better. The hero cycles, and epics in a sort of blank verse recitative, begin as a prose matrix for the song sequences by which mythical events and characters are celebrated, and take over the measure of the occasion by which they are celebrated. They are not found at all in the more primitive groups.

In other words, we do not discover poetry used by the Amerindian aboriginal for the purpose of conveying information. The informative use of drum tones among African savages suggests an earlier use of tonal quality for the same purpose. But the combination of voice and drum in the oldest Amerind usage is *never for any other purpose than that of producing and sustaining collective states.* Among primitives there is no other distinction between prose and poetry than this. Prose is the medium of communication, but Poetry is the mode of communion. How the one passes into the other as the speaker rises from the pitch of communicating his idea, to a state of spiritual communion with his audience, I have tried to show in the Gettysburg address.

You will find this passage from communication to communion affected more than once in the work of any natural orator. Somewhere along the rising tide of his eloquence, as ripples show on incoming water, rhythms recognized as prose begin to break into measures admittedly poetic. If he is not a born orator he will attempt, by the multiplication of adjectives and over-adornment of this thought by figures of speech, to accomplish the same thing. But he does not know any more than the Banderlog that what he is trying to accomplish is to lift the audience from states of detached cognition to states of collective realization. Here we have the secret of the love of the masses for high flowing wordiness. For, as the collective states are older, they are the more pleasurably entered into. As they are subjective, they are shorter cuts than the laborious paths of cognition, and by the release of associated emotional states, they provide an anodyne for the motor impulses. Or at the utmost, they make it possible to satisfy all such impulse with the minimum of expenditure. The difference between the mob-mindedness created by a modern agitator and the tribal-mindedness of the Corn Dance is the difference between rhythms that are merely poetic and those that are rhythms of poetry. It is the difference between rhythms that produce an emotional effect and those that are spiritually affective.

In so far as it is possible to establish a distinction so subtle, lying as it does in a dimension little explored by the psychologist, I wish to offer this as the true criterion of value among the new rhythmic modes through which the young genius of America is seeking expression. And I know of no better way of establishing a sense of values in this dimension than to describe the way in which they came to me through my study of the rhythmic modes of the aboriginal American.

III

§ 6

To understand how verse forms become fixed in tribal life we must go far enough back in the period of the Dawn Mind to be able to reject the Freudian premise [7] of the primacy of the sex urge and the hunger urge as factors of self-realization, and boldly assert that the absorbing business of the Dawn Man was the realization of himself in relation to the Allness.

The sex urge is seasonal,[8] the belly pull a short one from tide to receding tide. Down to the neolithic age as we know it in America, the food search had not yet taken on the vibration of perpetual anxiety. Hunting was still the perpetual sport, and the earliest agriculture was the occasion for the earliest form of what we now know as psychological drama. Stone Age men, who had no sense of private property in food, yielding the fruit of the bow to the common meal, had myth, ritual, pictorial art and complicated totemic organization. Among many of the American tribes it was a point of "Highness," if you heard some one eating in your house at night, not to strike a light, lest it prove to be your enemy and you be tempted to begrudge him the food, which might be all that you happened to have on hand. Back of that were the Days-of-the-New, in which, apparently, man ate happily whatever proved eatable. Among our own aboriginals there is still evidence of the annual mating. Once having mated or eaten, there were neither ritualistic nor economic considerations to keep the Dawn Man thinking about either between times. But the mystery of his man-ness was always with him. His ego gave him no rest, blundering about in the irradiated fog of the Dawn Mind, alternately falling over himself or stumbling against the Allness. How much was Allness and how much self? How much of selfness was there in this stream of incident originating in his environment, mysteriously attached to his own destiny, frightening and inexplicable as the can tied to the dog's tail? Clearly this was a matter that, until it was in some fashion settled, made of living a precarious business. He beat his breast over it. With his bare foot he stroked out on the bare earth the assurance of identity, the I—I—I of the dance proclaiming, as the Quipa put it, the essence-of-being-as-existent-in-humanity; and the others danced with him. For the first I of the man-thing was not the I of himself, but only of Us, mankind. If he danced the I-song in his loneness, it was to call to himself that other by which he is made more completely one in becoming not himself only.

Probably man first danced as the buck dances, and the pelican, from the recurrent seasonal urge, the intoxication of the sun coming up from the south and the new growth in the forest, when he was proud of himself or insolent with good feeding.

Thus he discovered that, by the making of rhythmic movements and noises, power comes. The senses are keyed up. That mysterious awareness of his prey, the instant intake and response to the environment, which is traceable to no discoverable sense, but is of the utmost importance to the hunting kind, appreciates. This is a state so satisfying that it invites repetition.

Man learned to resort to the dance when he felt help-less or fragmentary, when he felt dislocated in his uni-verse. As he learned to know such states of psychic com-pletion for states of power, he danced for the sake of the meal or the mate. Who can doubt that the Allness is moved by our singing, since it immediately begins to throb in us as the dance progresses? Will not the corn fill out in the ear even as the soul fills?

§ 7

In this fashion poetry was first sought deliberately for its affective values. The greater suggestibility of the Dawn Mind make it more than likely that though there must have been a first singer, the first song, the earliest remembered and reiterated pattern of thumps and vocables was communal.

We have here to take into account—later to come back to—the superior capacity of the Dawn Mind for mimesis. One observes it in the false dawn of the ape mind, the flock and the swarm. When one of the great males of the Dawn tribe beat upon his breast with rolling noises, the rest followed. Consciousness is beaten into synchronous waves by the rhythmic impact and the track of the first poetic line is laid in the group mind. The memory for these things in the group mind is more tenacious than in the mind of the individual. Every now and then when we run together under pressure of emotion, some hundred-thousand-year-old memory rises out of it to swamp all our recent acquirement.

§ 8

Within the territory of what is now the United States, the Amerind's highest literary culture was just about at the point at which, in Greek literature, the hero cycles were combined into the Homeric epic. But the greater part of what has survived the European invasion is much more primitive. It must not be assumed, however, that because primitive, it is necessarily simple. Psychologically the state called primitive is one of deeply imbricated complexity. If simple at all, only as the bud is simple within which are packed leaf and stem and flower. I find myself in difficulties at this point because the psychologists have failed to provide me with exact and discriminating terms in the very department with which the psychology of the hour concerns itself, the Deep-self, loosely described as the subconscious. If we had no other evidence of it, we should have to suppose a subconsciousness for poetry to come from, since it so obviously cannot be produced by effort of the intelligence. We should have no alternative otherwise than to suppose it whispered in the ear by the dæmon of the Greek, or to accept as veridical the Amerind's account of how certain of his song sequences were taught him in dreams by his Totemic Animal. But if we began by supposing that the part of the Amerind's mind from which his poetry comes is identical with the limbo of maimed impressions which the Freudian psychologist finds below the threshold of his contemporaries, we should be far from understanding him.

A primitive state of mind is, as nearly as I can make out, a state of acute, happy awareness. Streams of impressions of perennial freshness flow across the threshold of sense, distinct, unconfused, delicately registering, *unselected*. The exigencies of what we call civilization have forced upon us moderns a selective intensity of observation such as rarely occurs in primitive experience. An Amerind, no doubt, if he had to cross Fifth Avenue in the midst of traffic, in the absence of a traffic manager, would be constrained to the same concentration of passage which keeps us largely unaware of the color, the majesty, the multiplying rhythms of our streets. But in normal primitiveness the range of awareness is immensely extended and for the most part without egoistic or emotional connotation.

It is this impersonal extension of the faculty of awareness which has brought the Indian the reputation of superior sense perception, which is not borne out by scientific tests of sense reaction. The Indian sees no better than the white man, but he sees more, registers through every sense, some of which have atrophied in us, infinitely more. It is upon this enlarged reservoir of sensory impressions that he draws in his poetic dance dramas, every one of which comprises an orchestration of subjectively coördinated rhythms which the white man cannot always perceive and not easily resolve into mathematical indices. This appears to be true of all primitives. Charles Meyer relates how he saw a Malay drummer laughed out of the native orchestra for his failure to maintain a distinctive temporal relation with the *tawak,* which Meyer, himself a musician, failed to appreciate. We find vestiges of this coördination of, to our sense, unrelated rhythms in all Oriental music, and I have long suspected that certain early complexities of Greek lyric verse are survivals of the same primitive overlapping.

My own temporal perceptions are entirely inadequate to an estimate of the range of this capacity for combining dissimilar rhythmic series and regarding them as members of a complex unit. One winter at Tesuque I saw the Eagle dancers on a windy day catch up the

rhythm of the wind through the tips of their wing-
spread plumes and weave it into the pattern of their
ancient dance, to the great appreciation of the native
audience. After twenty years' observation, it remained
for Ovington Colbert, a Chickasaw, to point out to me
that the subtle wavering of the movement of the Squaw
Dance, which I had supposed to be due to the alternate
relaxation and tension of interest, was really responsively
attuned to the wind along the sagebrush.

But it is not only in respect to what comes to him
from the world outside that the awareness of the primitive exceeds the span of sophisticated attention. There
is even ground for supposing that the fringes of
his consciousness are lapped by ripples of energy that
proceed from the life process going on within himself and
that he attempts to exteriorize them in rhythmic movements or sounds produced by the orchestration of his
members. Once the tempo of the dance is established,
an Amerind audience will successfully subordinate the
distinctive rhythms set up by different parts of the body,
emphasized by rattles attached to body and members,
or as I have once seen it done, by a bandeau of whispering cocoons wrapped round the torso. The temporal rela-
tions of these embellishments are exceedingly subtle.
The tortoise shell rattle at the knee, for example, contributes two distinct elements, the shake which accom-
panies the thump of the foot and another following the
lift of the foot, rising to a point of silence and after a
dying fall, achieving silence once more just before the
foot touches the ground. The Amerind accomplishes
these things by virtue of that more intimate relation,

in primitive man, between the sensorimotor and the autonomic nervous systems, and by his superior faculty of mimesis. Just as children learning to talk will catch and perfectly repeat whole sentences not before heard, the primitive will seize upon complex rhythmic phrases, and, without any attempt to resolve them into their elements, reproduce them by the instrumentation of his members. Perception of rhythmic form in nature is driven so deeply into his subconscious, that in those dances where pure appreciation of his fortunate relation to Allness takes precedence of the ritualistic element, he can seize upon and coördinate with his dance the rhythm of sun, wind, or falling water, making himself part of the inextricable pattern of the hour.

It is probably the subconscious memory of the part played by all our members in this primitive coördination, that gives rise to the intricate variations and embellishments of Afro-American rhythms that go by the name of jazz,[9] rhythms that can only be successfully achieved by unharnessing the body from its civilized inhibitions. In any group of jazz performers you can see the arm jerk, recalling the tortoise rattle, the whole torso quiver with the remembered rolling clash of shells.

The Europeanly derived American is too far from this form of response to make it an item in his own scale of expression. But there can be no doubt that his subjective appreciation of rhythmic form has been immensely stimulated by the new motor complexes, and the stream of new rhythmic impressions flowing to him from the American scene. That some sort of subjective coördination of this immense complexity of impression is what

Whitman tried for, what Carl Sandburg, Vachel Lindsay
and Sherwood Anderson are occasionally succeeding at,
there can be, I think, no question. Whitman too often
failed at coördination, was reduced to mere end-to-end
notation.

The younger men, though confused with the loud
sound of unassimilated things, do better, confining themselves to naturally related groups of impressions. In
Vachel Lindsay there are points of simultaneity with the
rhythms of all deep forested river bottom lands in which
the Mississippi and the Congo have place and kinship.
In Anderson's early poems there is too much likeness to
the characteristic corn land movements not to have been
premeditated, except for the singular circumstance that
when I first noted such resemblances there were no accessible records of the corn dance movements for Mr.
Anderson to have imitated. And, if one could imagine
that the tribe of modern industrial workers had come
together for the purpose of promoting a communal attack
on the modern environment by means of rhythmic dance
drama, the rhythmic patterns would undoubtedly have
been the sort that Mr. Sandburg has produced in his
Smoke and Steel. But there would have been this difference between the dance drama of American life as
Mr. Sandburg records it and the dance drama of the
Amerind, that the Amerind admits none of the bond-
loosening, soul-disintegrating, jazz-born movements of
Mr. Sandburg's *Man Hunt*. Dance that rhythm tune in
your mind merely, letting the body respond as you will
feel it must to describe the rhythm adequately, and you

will see at once why its affectiveness would be toward spiritual disintegration. It would also be clear to you what Mr. Lindsay meant by "letting in the Congo, and Mumbo Jumbo."

I am not prepared to say that the Amerind never used rhythms of disintegration. One imagines the old Iroquois torture dances might have been of that description. Reports differ as to the affective quality of the phallic dances, which I have not seen. I am inclined, however, to accept the word of scientific observers that these are fertilization rites which have been allowed to lose their original religious character. They become what most poetry of the past few generations has been, effective rather than affective.

All this carries us very far from the academic notion of the "simple lyric cry" of primitive man. By our bookish habit of assuming that all the poetry of aboriginal song is in the words, we arrive at such utterly misrepresentative ideas of aboriginal simplicity.

Meumann, who has given much attention to this matter, seems to think that there is no such thing as simple rhythm, but that a "subjective binding together of impressions into a whole is inseparable from the simplest case of rhythmic perception." [10] The element of subjectivity must at least be present to produce an affective result. The Amerind has no system, of which he can give an account, of coördinating rhythmic impressions. I would say they are combined by the esthetic sense if I had not long ago come to the conclusion that there is no such sense existing apart, organically unrelated to any other sense. If there is an esthetic sense it must have some such function in consciousness as the sense of taste has in the physical organism. The esthetic sense might be to the development of the individual consciousness what the mouth is to the body, the threshold at which the esthetic experience is rendered poignant. If you will admit that there is such a thing as Mind, Psyche, "Entity X" of the psychophysicists, with its own mode of self-preservation and of self-realization—possibly of reproduction—then I will admit an esthetic sense as its mode of contact with experiences peculiar to Entity X. This leaves me free to admit that the esthetic sense is the coördinator for rhythmic perceptions, since it at the same time gives me leave to discuss the principle of coördination as a self-preservative procedure of the psyche.

The Amerind makes poetry because he believes it to be good for him. He makes it because he believes it a contribution to the well-being of his group. He makes it to put himself in sympathy with the *wakonda*, the *orenda* or god-stuff which he conceives to be to some degree in every created thing. Finally—and on almost every occasion—he makes it to affect objects that are removed from him in the dimension of *time and space*.

This affectiveness is secured by two processes, by the subjective coördination of the major rhythms involved, into a rhythmic unit, and the objective coördination of the movements involved, by mimesis. At the same time that the Amerind is using his body as an instrument of rhythm, he is using it as an instrument of realization of the result he desires to affect. He paints his body, decorates it with mimetic symbols, moves it through the phases of mimetic gesture, culminating in specific acts which are always mimetic even when least realized.

This mimesis is, as I understand it, the background of Aristotle's "imitation," which he regarded as the essential of poetry. Aristotle was near enough to this early source of tragic drama, which is what he always means when he speaks of poetry, to have realized it as an attempt to understand the Universe, to get inside it by doing as it does. This faculty of creative imitation must have been immensely more active in the Dawn Man than in us. One supposes a period of mimetic activity similar to the period of imitative articulation in children, by which they learn words at a more rapid rate than they are ever capable of in their later years. The Dawn Man did not understand rain as we understand it, but he had an acute power of appreciating all the visual and auditory accompaniments of rain, and of mimetically reproducing them. When he wished for rain, he set up within his own consciousness the utmost intensity of realization of rain of which he was capable. This is the content of Aristotle's "imitation," a "making" into which entered the three factors which are the essentials of Amerind verse: internal rhythms, coördinated by the prevailing motor habit; external rhythm subjectively coordinated; realization by means of creative mimesis. Or if we wish to present these factors in modern American terms we have, as the essentials of a genuinely native poetry; a motor habit set up by democratic, constructive labor; subjective coördination of the rhythmic forms of the American scene; realization of the meaning of the American experience in terms of activity.

§ 9

The Tribesmen used poetry as a means of raising the plane of group consciousness. Some method of doing this must have been indispensable to the upward movement of tribal life. The success of Democratic organization depends finally on the establishment among its members of a state of uncoerced obedience to its ideals. As early as the Dawn period, man had discovered the poetic orgy as the best means to this end. It is the only means that has ever been discovered of insuring the group mind, once the coalescence of individual minds has taken place, against those regressions which are always implied with us in the term, mob-mindedness.

Mob-mindedness can be produced by emotional impact on the uncoördinated group, lying easily at the mercy of suggestion which has no seat in the intelligence. It can be produced by a single leader to whom responsibility for leadership has already been transferred, or by one who wrests responsibility from a doubtful hour, and spreads by contagion. But affective group-mindedness has been arrived at only by a calculated participation of every individual in the group, in selected rhythmic performances. Some figment of the wisdom of our ancients remains with us to this day in our disposition to look with distrust on the single "agitator" whose method is of rhythmic impact on his audience, and to engage for

our important communal functions in an enfeebled practice of singing and band playing.

Fortunately modern psycho-physiology relieves me of
the necessity of demonstrating that the aboriginal poetic
orgy does have race-preserving values, in the energization of the sympathetic nervous centers. It is too often
forgotten in this connection that the Greek period of
the world's greatest florescence of intellect was one in
which rhythmic exercise was part of the accepted training
of youth, and participation in poetic orgies an item of
good citizenship.[11] What we have in the Amerindian
dance drama is the beginning of this most sophisticated
practice.

IV

§ 10

No final and authoritative study of Amerind verse has
yet been made. Before particularizing in the limited
field of my own inquiries, I must clear up certain mis-
understandings as to my connection with the whole subject of Amerindian life. Our easy newspaper habit of
ascribing authority where there is no more than an in-
formed and intelligent interest, has credited me with
being an authority on things Indian, which I am not,
as a translator which I never pretended to be, and as a
poet which I am only occasionally, and by induction.

When I say that I am not a translator, I mean that
I have not approached the work of giving English form

to Amerind songs by any such traditional literary posture as signalizes the work of Amy Lowell and Witter Bynner in making translations from the Chinese. If forced to affix a title to my work I should prefer to call it not translation, but re-expression. My method has been, by preference, to saturate myself in the poem, in the life that produced it and the environment that cradled that life, so that when the point of crystallization is reached, I myself give forth a poem which bears, I hope, a genetic resemblance to the Amerind song that was my point of contact.

These contacts began when, with the ink on my diploma scarcely dry, I was transplanted from a Middle Western college town to that portion of the American desert which I have described in *The Land of Little Rain* and *Lost Borders*. Here the problem of aboriginal life and its relation to the environment was the only meat upon which the avid appetite of youth could feed. I lapped up Indians as a part of the novelist's tormented and unremitting search for adequate concepts of life and society, and throve upon them.

I began by knowing a remnant of the evanished Mission San Gabriel group, then Yokuts, Paiutes, Washoes, Utes, Shoshones, and later enlarged my borders to include some acquaintance with Mojaves, Pimas, Papagoes, Mescalero Apaches, Tewas, Taos, and an occasional individual Plainsman. Better than I knew any Indian, I knew the land they lived in. This I hold to be a prime requisite for understanding originals of whatever description. It was only by such familiarity with the condition under which a land permits itself to be lived

with that I was able to overcome the difficulty of language.

All the great divisions of Amerind speech differ among
themselves more than the root languages of Europe, and
they possess an infinity of dialects.   There are, however, tribesmen who take a pride in the number of native
languages to which they can set their tongues, and others
who speak fair English and Spanish.   Though I have
no "ear" for language, I have an exceedingly quick sense
of language structure, and the underlying thought pattern of all Amerind tongues is the same.   Moreover, the
Amerind himself is of a scholarly turn of mind, and once
he is convinced of the high ground of your interest, he
will unwearyingly hunt down for you the last fugitive
syllable of elucidation.   Sitting on the sunny side of the
wickiup, considering with the elders of Sagharewite how
it came to be called the Place-where-they-gave-him-
mush-that-was-afraid, I thought of doctors disputing in
the temple, of academicians loitering amid olive groves,
and occasionally I thought of the Ancient Mariner.   For
when you have invited a strange people to unfold their
mysteries you must by no means show yourself bored by
the unfoldment.

The effect of all this, the only intellectual life I was
to have for sixteen years, on my own mind and its output
is probably more extensive than I have been able to
reckon.   It has given to my literary style its best thing, a
selective economy of phrase, and its worst, a habit of
doubling an idea back into its verbal envelope so that
only the two ends of it stick out, which to this day I
labor in vain to eradicate.   Its total effect was to con-

vince me, as I think every one does become convinced
who lives sincerely among Indians, that the earliest suf-
fusing flush of human consciousness under a sense of its
relation to the Allness is immensely more important to
our social solutions than our far derived culture of the
universities has permitted us to realize. So, from the
first, my quest was for primitive concept, for folk-
thought under folk-ways. In the beginning, form interested me so little that I did not even undertake to
record the original form of the songs I collected, stripping
it off as so much husk, to get at the kernel of experience. Somewhere in print I have said that women as
a class are indifferent to form. Take it that I was
then behaving in a characteristically feminine way, but
do not forget that the university had not taught me to
recognize literary quality in any form of which the
original mold was not Greek or Roman or Hebrew.
It was not until I found my own unpremeditated songs
taking the Amerind mold that I realized what I had
stumbled upon.

You must not suppose, however, that all this time
I had been confining my inquiries to mere verbal transliterations of legend and song. I have naturally a
mimetic temperament which drives me toward the understanding of life by living it. If I wished to know
what went into the patterns of the basket makers, I
gathered willows in the moon of white butterflies and
fern stems when these were ripest. I soaked the fibers
in running water, turning them as the light turned, and
did my ineffectual best to sit on the ground scraping
them flat with an obsidian blade, holding the extra

fibers between my toes. I made singing medicine as I
was taught, and surprised the Friend-of-the-Soul-of-
Man between the rattles and the drums. Now and then
in the midst of these processes I felt myself caught up
in the collective mind, carried with it toward states of
super-consciousness that escape the exactitudes of the
ethnologist as the life of the flower escapes between the
presses of the herbalist. So that when I say that I am
not, have never been, nor offered myself, as an authority
on things Amerindian, I do not wish to have it understood that I may not, at times, have succeeded in being
an Indian.

§ 11

I do not recall, except as I have already suggested,
when, and by what steps I began to see that what was
true of the earliest poetic expression of the American
spirit must be largely true of all such expression. I
think the experiences of coming into touch with the
beginning poetry and the becoming poetry of America
were part of one process. The arc of my mind has an
equal swing in all directions. I should say the same of
your mind if I thought you would believe it. But we
are so saturated with the notion that Time is a dimension
accessible from one direction only, that you will at first
probably be shocked by my saying that I can see truly
as far in front of me as I can see exactly behind me.
We all of us come out of school with our heads canted
over one shoulder at that portion of the trail from which
we lately emerged. We do not even see that clearly, but

crowded with shadow pictures thrown there by those who have taken it upon themselves to determine what is good for us to see. So when we at last find ourselves fronting the future, we see there only phantasmagoria, the reflection of a reflection, or at best the projection of unrelated fancy. But if we can, by hook or crook, get into a veridical stream of tendency; if we feel ourselves carried by it as it moves forward from clearly perceived sources, then—and perhaps you will admit this of your own mind now that you understand what I mean by it— we shall have no difficulty in perceiving *along* the stream of tendency to its logical goal.

I, at any rate, became convinced as early as the first years of the present century, that American poetry must inevitably take, at some period of its history, the mold of Amerind verse, which is the mold of the American experience shaped by the American environment.

As I recall it, my first public expression of this conviction was in the winter of 1904-05, before the English Club of Stanford University. Afterward at other places, where it will still be remembered, because nobody at that time believed it. Our culture, stiffened into the Victorian gesture of giving, received nothing from the self-contained culture of the aboriginal. When I attempted to sell some of my reëxpressed Amerindian airs, not only did the *Atlantic Monthly* disdain to "see any excuse for this sort of thing!" but so widely read an editor as Richard Watson Gilder returned my verses with the suggestion that some of them might be published on their merit as verse, provided the author would frankly admit their authorship.

Two or three years later, less pretentious magazines like *McClure's* and *Everybody's* began to print not only my translations, but others. In the winter of 1910-11, The Poetry Society took notice to the extent of inviting me to address them on the subject. From every quarter spontaneous experiments in the new form made their appearance, more often than not without any acquaintance with the aboriginal forms. We were beginning to speak of the new medium as *vers libre*. But even so late as 1911, when my play, *The Arrow Maker,* what was left of it after a New York production, finally appeared in print, I had too little confidence in being understood to attempt to restore even the original form, much less the aboriginal type of free measures in which it was written.

Since the publication in 1916 of Mr. Cronyn's anthology of American Indian verse, and the fragments of my introduction which survived the process, interest in aboriginal forms has been more general. I doubt if any one now would venture, as one critic did on the appearance of that volume, to protest against Amerindian verse being "made to look like free verse," or with another, insist that it could not be imagistic, since Imagism is the exclusive product of the sophisticated imagination.

§ 12

It ought not to be necessary to justify the relationship between Amerind and American verse, seeing how completely we have accepted the involvement of Hellenic and Pelasgian influences in the best of Greek literature. Nobody denies the intermingled strains of British, Celtic and mixed Nordic elements in the best of English, or refuses to see the "Urdummheit," or primal stupidity, of the aboriginal Teuton informing the literature of Germany. But I have found intellectual Americans generally baulking at the idea that there could be any informative relation between their own present or future culture and the many thousand-year-old culture of the race that we displaced.

There is crass and inexcusable ignorance among our intellectuals of these things, and in our universities the traditional preoccupation with Greek and Roman antiquities leaves no attention free for equivalent phrases of cultural assimilation going on between our own Achaioi and Barbaroi.

It is probably not too much to say that all verse forms which are found worthy the use of great poets are aboriginal, in the sense that they are developed from the soil native to the culture that perfected them. Certainly this is true of the Greek forms in which the best examples of the later English poets are cast. The relation of Greek meters to Greek rites and dances is a matter of common scholarship, but the sacred character imputed to the rhythms and verse arrangements of the Old Testament has served to screen their derivation. That the meditative measures and slow, shepherd pacing rhythms of the Hebrews originated among cultures that were in many respects inferior to the cultures of some of our Amerind tribes, is an item that too often escapes consideration. That the Israelites, at the time that their psalm singing took the final forms so venerated by us, practiced polygamy and the ceremonial eating of flesh, and hewed their enemies in pieces before the Lord, there is not the slightest doubt. Under the pure lilt of Keats and Shelley it is still possible to follow the patter of naked feet in dances that may no longer be described with propriety, or in rituals in which living beasts were torn apart.

Not to know these things is to admit yourself unschooled in poetic origins. But the manner in which classic English verse is presented in universities, where most people first hear of it, rising on the intellectual horizon of youth like a golden cloud, makes every comparison between it and the verse forms of American Indians strike on its admirers as an offense.

In the common esteem, not only are the only good aboriginals dead ones, but all aboriginals are either sacred or contemptible according to the length of time they have been dead. The very word, aboriginal, comes in for a certain reprobation because of its more general use in connection with primitive cultures, so that it becomes necessary to explain that there may arise literary forms which are far from primitive without being any the less aboriginal. It is possible to find in the history of English verse up to the beginning of the American era, overlappings and interweavings of aboriginal Anglo-Saxon and British forms, struggling with and being on the whole out-climbed and smothered by the Greek aboriginals, kept alive by the sedulous classicism of the schools. It does not seem likely that this can happen in America. The extraordinary, unpremeditated likeness between the works of such writers as Amy Lowell,

Carl Sandburg, Vachel Lindsay and Edgar Lee Masters,
exhibiting a disposition to derive their impulses from
the gestures and experiences enforced by the American
environment, to our own aboriginals, points away from
any such usurpation by the Greek and Hebrew aboriginals.   At this hour of relaxed effort in Europe, the
American gesture promises to become dominant as the
mold of literary form.

§ 13

All Amerind poetry, even the most personal, presents
itself as three-plied movement and melody and words.
When the expression is communal, the movement and
instrumented rhythm may be of a complexity rivaling the
harmonic intricacies of a modern orchestra.   Witnessing
the Corn Dance of the Rio Grande Pueblos, one realizes
how it was that Aristotle came to treat of Poetry as
comprising several arts which we now think of as distinct
from it.   The Corn Dance is an affective fertility rite,
designed to bring rain and good growing weather to the
sprouting crops.   The dancers will number among the
hundreds, according to the population of the community.
The natural rhythm of their timing feet will run from
the pound of the men's thick soles, through the softer
shuffle of the women to the patter of children tailing out
the procession around the plaza, rising and falling and
overlapping like a musical round, bound together but
not necessarily synchronized by the beat of the tombes,
steady and quick like the heart of the sun beating.   In
and out of these primary rhythms play the body accents,

knee rattle and arm rattle of deer's hoofs or tortoise case, and the lovely silver clash of the wreathes of conus shells about the glistening torsos of the men. From point to point, like the rush of summer rain, runs the roll of prisoned pebbles in the hand-held gourds. All the dancers sing, moving deftly in their places from time to time as the orchestral pattern of the rhythm requires. Out and aside the elders sing, prayerfully, inviting the coöperation of the People of Middle Heaven in rhythms that are not necessarily temporally synchronous, though subjectively coördinated with the song of the dancers.

To this will be added the symbolically painted bodies and faces, the intricate mimetic symbolism of costume and decoration, and at selected intervals mimetic presentations of the drama of the Corn. Out of some such many stranded cord was spun the Poetics of Aristotle. By means of it the Dawn Man drew the Seven Arts out of his own entrails.

As I have already tried to show, the relation of gesture to poetry is generative. By means of the provocative rhythms of foot and drum, the autonomic centers are aroused and the collective consciousness set in motion; on the crests of its movement poetic realizations arise as the foam-cap on waves.

Of the dance then, only so much is necessary to be taken into the poetic record of aboriginal experience as serves to indicate the determining urge; of supplication, of triumph, of abasement. But here I should have to warn the researcher whose only access to aboriginal life is by way of the printed page, that much of our descriptive phraseology is misleading. A war dance may not be for the purpose of inciting a warlike spirit, but a prayer to the Twins of War and Chance for peace and protection. A scalp dance is not necessarily an expression of ferocious triumph, but a ritual of adoption of the *manes* of the dead into our tribe. It is reported that the last dance of this character took place three years ago in a secret place in the southwestern hills around four blond scalps, designed to make peace and kinship between our own dark soldiers and the ghosts of the Germans they had slain—may it prove efficacious!

Mistakes of this character were made more than once by Burton, who studied his Ojibway music from the life, and yet persisted in treating songs of mystical seeking, such as are common in all aboriginal groups, as personal love songs of a sweetish sentimentality. It is to avoid such errors that I confine my own work to reëxpressions of the songs of familiarly known tribes.

Once the fundamental rhythm is established, for the contributory rhythms the translator may take as many as he can successfully handle. No one has handled these secondary rhythms with absolute success, though Lew Sarrett gives evidence of appreciating them, and Carl Sandburg certainly could do it if he set himself to such an undertaking. Of the mimesis, both in acts and in all the finely divided symbolism of color and face painting and ornament, I should use in reëxpression as much as is descriptively an aid to realization. It is a nice point to determine just when a feathered stick, a headdress or a girdle is properly an item of poetic realization, and when it is to be relegated to the department of stage setting; but this is not to be compared for difficulty to the dividing of the two twined cord of words and melody.

They appear to be evoked simultaneously in the mind of a poet. At first glance the melody would seem most important; not only the melodic line, but the rhythmic pattern of melodic elements, for the words can be easily shown to adapt themselves to the melody, even by the use of such variation as goes by the name of poetic license with us. There is also visible filling out of the melodic pattern by meaningless vocables. But a long study of Amerindian modes of thought convinces me that there are differences in the way in which poems come into existence which must govern the method of translation.

We have to bear in mind that melody had to do all the work for the primitive that is done now with print, with punctuation and capitals and italics, with visual arrangement of line and stanza. In other words, melody is the mold of form, the matrix of stanza arrangement. Melody therefore cannot be neglected in lyric translation. It is full of interesting suggestion of pattern development, and a study of melodic pattern correlated with decorative pattern among the same people should prove of value. The reason why you do not find more of it in my own work is that I am temperamentally less interested in the purely lyric aspects of poetry. Nevertheless I have given one or two examples of it in *The Heart's Friend,* which was my first translation, and in the *Sioux Song at Parting,* which reproduces the melodic pattern of the original without variation.

For perfect examples of this type of aboriginal ex-

pression, see the work of Natalie Curtis Burlin. Mrs.
Burlin had a lyric intuition which makes her translations
so many clear markers on the road to the spring of
native inspiration, and her untimely death is an irre-
parable loss to us.

Alice Fletcher in her admirable work on the *Hako*
ceremony has attempted lyric translations of the whole
sequence. One feels certain that if an Americanly edu-
cated Indian had been translating the *Hako* he would
have done it in just that way. Thinking of it as a thing
to be sung, he would find it subject to the necessity of
music to account for every fraction of time within the
melodic measure. Understanding that in English poetry
every syllable must seem to mean something, whether it
does or not, he would have replaced the vocables in the
melodic pattern with words, just as Miss Fletcher has
done. The result is a remarkable rendering in words of
melodic mimesis, following the very shapes of the land
and the movements by which the ritual is accomplished.

One cannot help thinking that an Indian poet without
any knowledge of classic English forms would have pro-
ceeded very differently. Concerned only to render true
poetic values, this hypothetical aboriginal translator—
who, except for two or three examples furnished by
Charles Eastman in precisely this manner, has not yet
appeared—would know that the extra syllabication
served no purpose but to fill out the melodic pattern, and
that most of the repetitions were purely ritualistic in
character, having reference to the magic properties of
song and in general determined by the sacred tribal number. These he would therefore largely omit. If used at

all, it would only be to establish the fundamental rhythm of the experience that provoked the poetic explosion. Such a translator's first care, then, would be to state the experience itself, usually by stating its most important reaction on himself. To this he would add no more than he found absolutely necessary by way of descriptive and associative phrases, to define the path of the experience through his own consciousness.

Now this is precisely the way the primitive, when he first arrives at writing, begins to evolve what is called a glyph. If he wishes to state that in the year of fire-coming-out-of-the-mountain, the great chief died, first he draws a man and over him places the symbol of chiefhood. Close by he draws a mummy or burial urn or other index of our common end, accompanied by a pictorial suggestion of the way in which the death was accomplished, if this happens to be important, and finally, in an upper corner, the mountain belching fire. Around the whole, binding them irrevocably to a single effort of attention, he draws a line.

It is probable that the melodic line serves something of the same purpose in Amerindian verse, giving whole-ness to the emotional and esthetic contributions.

For an instance of the same process in another medium, examine the Thunderbird design which decorates this cover, reproduced from a ceremonial bowl unearthed in one of the pre-Columbian pueblos. Within the circle fixed by the bowl's proportions, we have not a drawing of a bird, but an adequate suggestion of birdness, of birdness the most majestic, whose wings are made of the dark cloud, whose feathers are edged with the dark mist, presiding over fertility provoking storms, and hence also the presiding genius of power-inducing song.

But there is more in this headless design of wing and tail spread, which is the figure of any great bird seen from below, high-flying. There is the primitive's prayerful attitude toward it, which is cunningly expressed in the stepped altar design, the earth-altar line of the desert horizon, worked into the tail-spread until it also contributes to the feather suggestion of the design. At the top, inside the wing-spread, are the full curved clouds like breasts, and the three straight strokes of falling rain.

In this fashion the Thunderbird, his function, the attitude of the artist and his faith, are expressed in lines, which in the original being black and white on a red earth ground, give a note of the play of light and dark between earth and heaven in the process of the storm. In this fashion also the two arts of writing and pictorial representation began. A little more detail would have made a picture of a Thunderbird, a little less and we should have had an ideograph for thunderstorm.

In this collection the song called *The Magic Ribbon* is the best example of the primitive process of poetic realization. Washoe Charlie's girl had gone away to Indian Board School and Charlie had given her a grass-green hair ribbon for remembrance. A few days later, while his loss was sorest, he had a glimpse of another girl wearing an identical green ribbon. Any lover will understand what happened to Charlie, though as he expressed it in the song recording the experience, whole, as it occurred to him, there were only half as many words as I have put into it:

"The Green ribbon, when I saw a girl wearing it, my girl existed inside me." One touch more Charlie added by calling his song the magic ribbon. The rest any Washoe was supposed to understand by the likeness of all Washoe lovers one to another.

Stephen Crane has left us no note of what happened to him in the neighborhood of Yellow Sky to explain how he happened to write, "If I should cast off this tattered coat," and

> "I looked here
> I looked there
> Nowhere could I see my love,
> And—this time—
> She was in my heart.
> Truly then, I have no complaint,
> For though she be fair and fairer,
> She is not so fair as she
> In my heart."

Yet in writing thus he was nearer the poetic modes of the Rio Grande country than any white man has been since. At that time, however, when I was exchanging songs with Washoe Charlie, I had not come across the Black Riders.

§ 14

It is this similarity of primary processes which has led me to adopt the term "glyph" for a type of Amerind song which is lyric in its emotional quality and yet cannot be completely expressed by the simple lyric cry.

Experience presents itself as One; existing by itself in

Consciousness. The experience completely transpires; the autonomic centers are stirred, giving rise to motor impulses. Rhythm ensues and with rhythm the esthetic sense is quickened, evoking order and arrangement. Words are perhaps the final evocation of the intelligence, taking possession of the experience and decorating it appropriately.

It is here, in the verbal realization, that we come upon the common root of aboriginal and modern Americanness.

We have seen how native rhythms develop along the track of the rhythmic stimuli arising spontaneously in the environment and are coördinated by the life-sustaining gestures imposed upon us by that environment. Although we have not yet achieved the communality into which the Amerind has entered by easy evolution, there is evident straining toward it in the work of such men as Masters, Frost and Sandburg; all our recent poetic literature touched with a profound nostalgia for those happy states of reconciliation with the Allness through group communion, which it is the business of poetry to promote.

It is not surprising then, that with this common urge toward communality, with this shared stream of rhythmic stimuli proceeding from the environment, and the common similarity of gesture, that there should be a tendency toward similarity of form between the early and later American poets.

The disposition of the aboriginal poet is to arrange his words along what, for want of a better term, I have called the landscape line, the line shaped by its own inner necessities.

I must make a point of insisting upon this, since there is among translators a contrary disposition to insist upon the melodic line as the mold of aboriginal verse form. It is difficult to see just how they can ignore the universal aboriginal practice of completing the melodic line with repetitions of the felicitous phrases or by sheer meaningless syllabication, rather than force the meaning with added words, as our classic poets are obliged to do, or to pad it with adjectives until it fills out every accent of the musical measure. I have often read my translations to the aboriginal singer, and almost always with the result of cutting the verbiage back to its primitive austerity. I have had Indians try out my renderings to drum beats, by intervals evidently satisfactory to themselves, but often beyond my power to coördinate. I have sometimes had them insist on repetitive patterns. I have talked with aboriginal singers who seemed to distinguish between repetitive recurrence of a rhythmic pattern which was purely esthetic, and repetition which was magical, determined by the sacred tribal number. But I have never met with the slightest disposition to force the words into a predetermined mold. Mold or rhythm-pattern, so far as it exists for the aboriginal exists only as a point of rest for the verse to flow into and out of as a mountain stream flows in and out of ripple-linked pools. It is this leap of the running stream of poetic inspiration from level to level, whose course cannot be determined by anything except the nature of the ground traversed, which I have called the landscape line. The length of the leaps, and the sequence of pattern recurrences will be conditioned by the subjectively coordinated motor rhythms associated with the particular emotional flow.

This landscape line may of course involve several verse lines as they appear on the printed page, and is best described by the modern term, cadenced verse. In the placing of this line, and the additional items by which it is connotated and decorated, the aboriginal process approaches closest to what is known as Imagism, unless you will accept my term and call it glyphic. Once having adopted a definite space of consciousness for the purpose of realizing it poetically, the supreme art of the Amerind is displayed in the relating of the various elements to the central idea. Like his cognate, the Japanese, the Amerind excels in the art of occupying space without filling it. Sometimes the whole area of experience is sufficiently occupied by a single undecorated statement, as in this Chippewa:

> As my eyes search the prairie
> I seem to see the summer in the spring,

or in this which is sung by the Pawnee when he takes the war trail at the end of which death may await him:

> Let us see;
> Is it real,
> This life which I am living?

Here we have a direct poetic perception threading the objectivity of experience delicately as an owl flits, without once brushing it with the down-edged tip of its wings. But in this introductory phase of a Pima sequence the object of the song is not stated, though to

the Piman mind the course of its flight is perfectly indicated:

> Thence I run, in flickering darkness,
> Wearing bisnaga blossoms in my hair
> Thence I run, as darkness gathers,
> In vibrant darkness, to the singing place.

By this suggestion of flight through the vibrating twilight of spring in Arizona, the singer indicates and aug-
ments the flight of his soul toward the secret place from
which song-magic springs. In the best Amerindian
poetry the object is absorbed into the singer and is
seldom seen except as a link in the chain, completing
the circuit of interest between the object and his own
breast.

Thus poetry becomes the means by which men and
their occasions are rewoven from time to time with the
Allness; and who is there to tell me that this, in art, is
not the essence of modernity?

§ 15

It will readily appear that what I have worked out
so far refers rather to aboriginal modes of poetic realization than to literary form. I have already explained
that this is partly owing to a lack of lyric interest on
my part, and partly to my having, very early in my
search turned aside into a particular inquiry about the
use of rhythm as a medium for what we have generally
agreed to call poetic drama. The results of this inquiry
I hope to develop fully in a later volume on the *American*

Gesture. It would be a mistake, however, for the reader to infer from my work that I have done more than make temperamental selections from the rich variety of literary forms which the aboriginal himself has worked upon the warp of native rhythms.

Historically these should be studied backward from about the point at which Greek forms begin with definiteness to issue. Here you will find every stage of stanza development, assonance, emphatic rhyme, internal rhyme, decorative repetition, incremental repetition, and refrain.

In ritualistic sequences, such as the *Hako* and the *Night Chant,* will also be found more than a suggestion of formal progression of rhythmic modes such as we recognize as underlying symphonic composition. I know of no better contribution to the science of poetics than could be made by setting all this material in order. In the meantime I make my own small contribution by setting down two or three of the conclusions I have come to about particular problems arising out of the effort to reëxpress Amerindian poetry in American values.

In discarding ritualistic repetitions and syllabication which is shown to be mere stuffing of the melodic pattern, one must not overlook the values they may have as stage setting, or as indices of the emotional values. One must have seen the women genuflect in response to the wild cries which swoop and flit like hawks above a Pueblo war dance to realize that these are not mere whoops of ebullient savagery, but prayers to the Twins of War and Chance, charged with the values of such worshipful responses as Lord Have Mercy on Us, or **Hear Thy People, Lord!** Many of the apparently meaningless or obsolete words in primitive poetry probably had similar significances.

Since all the aboriginal singer's contacts with his subject are experiential, his poetic values are often so personal that they would be largely missed by the stranger to his way of life if it were not that he seldom fails to provide somewhere in the rhythm, in the onomatopoetic syllabication or in some apparently unrelated phrase a key to the song's objectivity. This will generally be indicated by the singer's reluctance, which is frequently inhibitory, to sing the song without this accompaniment. It is, for instance, very difficult for the young men of Taos to render the Moon Song without rising to stand in a row as if on the bridge between the Summer and Winter Houses, facing in that quarter from which the mistress of the night sky issues. In the case of communal song sequences the stage setting may be a complicated mimetic ritual. But whenever you find an Indian unwilling to sing a particular song without its accompanying act, that act is an essential item of the song's meaning and must be so translated. That is why you will often find my own translations so much longer than the original words seem to warrant.

§ 16

One of the most usual mistakes made by beginners in this field, is that of assuming that because Amerindian culture is primitive, all expressions of it must be in words of one syllable.

It must be remembered in this connection that the

genius of Amerind speech is holophrastic. **Every im-**
portant word is a fist well fingered with syllables **not**
one of which can be omitted without maiming the concept implicit in the word. I know a place in the Tejon
called by a word of which the full unfolding was fear-
living-in-that-place-shakes-continually. No mere English equivalent such as quicksand or quaking bog could
convey all that was in the namer's mind any more than
the outline of a fist would measure all the spread hand
might hold. The translator's problem, then, is not one
of simplification, but of achieving a deeply imbricated
wholeness.

The rhythms of holophrastic words occur in natural
clusters; rhythm seems often to be the principle of organization, so that, in spite of the clicks and gutturals
that characterize many Amerind tongues, one finds such
lovely words as *tchu-pa-tchu-ti, hi-mo-va'-li, tse'-yan-a-
tho"-ni,* and *te-jo-ska-wa-ye'n-ton.* Cadences like these
cannot easily be represented in the Wordsworthian aus-
terities that some critics have mistakenly insisted should
replace them. At the same time it is important to avoid
violating the stricture that Kern River Jim used to make
against white men's songs, that they "talked too much."
The translator will have to put more into his words than
the Amerind expressed by them, but he must not put
everything in

No Indian ever says all his thought. Always there
is some petal left furled, some secret untransfixed to be
exhaled as a delicate perfume upon the inner sense.
"You see Piuty man singin' sometime, and cryin' when
he sing," says Kern River Jim, "it ain't what he singin'

make him cry. It's what he thinkin' about when he sing make him cry."

I have always felt at liberty to put into my versions all that I could discover of what the singer was thinking about. In the song for the Passing of a Beautiful Woman I have tried not to ladyfy the thought, though there was a patent difficulty in getting it clearly expressed by the singer, who complained that though the original was not considered a bad song, all the "White man's words" available "mean bad." That means of course that our schools have never taught the Indian any words for love that have not the stamp of baseness. It was to be expected of a people who would undertake to insist that the Corn Dance should be danced in pajamas, lest Deity, to whom the dance is made, should not be able to endure the sight of the bronzed thighs and shoulders he has given to the least of his Americans.

§ 17

It can not escape the attention of the prosodist that I have nowhere touched upon the problem of accent. There are two reasons for such an omission, the first being that accent does not appear to have any place in Amerind poetry apart from the natural movements of thought, and the accents of the language in which the original occurs. When you consider that the fifty-eight linguist groups of aboriginal American speech differ among themselves as much as the languages of Europe, and that only a few of their many dialectic variations have been recorded, you will readily see that no study of speech accents would have any weight in literary translations.

There are of course definite melodic accents which belong to the study of music, and do not seem to be carried over to verbal renderings by the Indians themselves. Nor have I, in all my experiments, been able to discover that the aboriginal derived any pleasure from metrical accent as we practise it. And of fundamental metrical accents, occurring in the major rhythms of the poetic dance, I would almost go so far as to say that there are none.

I am even inclined to insist that the temporal division of drum beats found in most recorded Amerind music is purely subjective, growing out of the inability of the sophisticated ear to hear without accent, and the necessity of notating aboriginal music in terms of which accent is an inescapable condition.

To account for my assurance on this point I must go back to the traditional pyrrhic meter of the archaic Greek period, in which the drum and foot beats are regularly spaced and unaccented, like stepping stones upon which the melody runs and leaps and pirouettes. This undifferentiated dub dub dub dub of the tombes which can be heard in the kivas of the Rio Grande Pueblos for days before the dance begins, is the most exhilarating sound in the world, and destroys at once the assumption that accent arises primarily in the effort of the listener to relieve the strain by setting up accents as points of rest. For this unaccented beat is so native to our inner selves that I have never heard even the most sophisticated complain of it; whereas the reiterated *One* two three, *One* two three of a modern drum, endured for so long would drive an ordinary person insane.

I do not say that examples of what might be called metrical accent may not yet be found in aboriginal dance, but the enormous preponderance of the unaccented beat forces us to conclude that it is not only older, but probably the oldest form of rhythm. Thus we are driven back on one or two assumptions. Either we are wrong in concluding that the compensating arrangement of one strong beat against two or three weak beats originates in man's right and left-handedness, or there was a time in his history when right and left-handedness had not yet been established as the prevailing mode. And this is precisely what seems to be the case.

Practically all authorities are agreed that the variability between dextrality and sinistrality decreases as we go backward in the history of the race. Now comes M. Sarafin, the eminent French archeologist, to say that a study of Neolithic remains in Europe convinces him that up to the beginning of the bronze age, European man had equal, interchangeable use of both hands. This is excellent ground for supposing that European aboriginals expressed themselves in unaccented rhythms similar to those used by aboriginal man in America, the last vanishing echo of which down the Greek vista caught, and may as well retain, the name of pyrrhic.

This helps us to fix the origin of accent as a device for establishing temporal coincidences, in man's growing disposition toward compensating bilaterality. The center of gravity of the body, a little to the right of the median line, becomes the point toward which is established that necessity of poetic rhythm to return upon itself, which Miss Lowell has pointed out. This we shall have to take up again in *The American Gesture*. It concerns our study of aboriginal rhythms only so far as it helps to define accent in poetry as a subjective attempt of the organism to handle series of undifferentiated stimuli, such as the *chuff chuff* of a steam engine, in terms of its own right and left-handedness. That the struggle is to establish balance is further shown by experiments recently undertaken in American laboratories, which indicate that even in the freest free verse there is a subjective disposition to set up temporal equivalence between a single strong and many weak syllables.

Evidently verse is never freed from man's struggle to come out even with himself . . . unless, of course, we are to accept some puzzling modern rhythms as the first attempt to record machine-handedness which may turn out to be as different from two-handedness as simple dextrality is from ambi-dextrality. Wherever man goes and *how*ever, the Muses must of necessity, come dancingly along beside him.

§ 18

I would unfairly conclude this record of my work if I omitted to return acknowledgments for the help I have had from the ethnological studies of such scholars as Fletcher and Densmore, Goddard and Boaz and Kroeber, Mathews and Cushing and Harrington. In admitting the contribution of their scholarship, I should fall short if I did not also acknowledge the generosity of their personal assistance in elucidating the creative process as it exhibits itself in the aboriginal mind.

Though they do not always take me so seriously as I take them, it would be unfair not to admit that they always take me good-humoredly. That I should make mistakes in a field where so little had been done before me was to have been expected.[12] That the only mistake I have ever had publicly to correct came of my trusting to the ethnologists too implicitly is my excuse for occasionally venturing beyond their findings on ground where nobody but a poet could have ventured at all.

Nor must I omit to say that I have frequently been made aware of my own poetic limitations. A better poet would have done better both by you and the Indian, but at the time most of this work was attempted, no better poet had offered. Practically all of this work had been done by 1910 and much of it published before 1914, about which time the free versifiers burst upon the world with loud cries of self-discovery. Both *Fire* and *The Arrow Maker* had been written, produced and published before there was any popular name by which to call the new form, and it is this priority of my experiment over much which has since captured the acclaim of critics which seems to justify this republication in collected form as part of the history of what has now proved to be a veridical American movement.

ADDENDA
FOR THE SECOND EDITION

INTRODUCTION

IN preparing an enlarged edition of the American Rhythm, the author, although for the eight years between it and the first, constantly in touch with the material, enlarging the borders of observation, finds nothing to add to the fundamentals upon which this study is based. The diffusion of information as to the make-up of the personal instrument, particularly as to the rhythmic concomitant of the endocrine glands, and the development of a competent vocabulary for the discussion of these things, has added much to the content of the reading mind. So that, although nothing of note has come recently from the laboratories in which rhythm has been studied, the general approach to what has already been learned has been so far popularized that it does not seem necessary to modify the summary of rhythm as it is generally agreed upon, with which the first edition opens. That rhythm is the fundamental mode of thought and emotion, perhaps the very mode of consciousness itself, is so generally conceded, that the least observant reader, not always able to trace the sources of particular rhythmic manifestations, can recognize them readily enough when pointed out. Suggestions such as that the rhythm of popular social dancing is referable to the increase of machine-handedness, in a world in which there are as many left turns as right, or that the body pivot for such dancing is to be found where the exigencies of the steering wheel locate it, about the middle of the spinal axis, provoke no more than a smile of amused acquiescence. Moreover, the growing interest of Americans in Amerind dancing, makes possible the instant recognition of similarities — such as the control of modern dance movement by the torso and the reduction of the legs to the purely utilitarian function of carrying the dancer about and, occasionally, serving as instruments of rhythm and accent. Even in what is known as esthetic dancing to-day, there is an emergence of the feeling for the body as mechanism, and a tendency for the abstraction of movement, out of the flowing lines of naturalism popularized by Isadora Duncan, toward the fundamental forms of matter, the majesty and power of the Universe machine. One observes this tendency notably in all the plastic arts, which are not burdened, as literature often is, with the necessity of conveying a certain amount of information. This is particularly true of the poets who, like T. S. Eliot, E. E. Cummings, Ezra Pound, D. H. Lawrence, and Robinson Jeffers, do not spare to carry the poetic adventure into dimensions heretofore preëmpted by philosophy and mathematics. With the growing conformity of the work of poets such as Sandburg, Frost, and Lindsay to the enclosing "landscape line" of their own quarter of Earth horizon, there seems to be no particular reason for stressing the American scene as the dominant of rhythmic expression in the United States.

§ 19

At the same time there has been a widespread acceptance of the interest and charm of Amerind verse.   Not that anybody has appeared willing to devote the profound and meticulous attention to it that is, in our Universities, being exercised on behalf of the combed over remains of early European folk poetry, but there is a notable increase of the number of persons willing to rework the carefully collected and literally translated product of the Bureau of Ethnology into marketable shape.   There are also poets like Lou Sarett and Witter Bynner and D. H. Lawrence who, having given themselves to living on Indian earth, are willing to admit the influence on their own output, of so fresh and vigorous a poetic approach.   But there is little actual original research being done.   With the exception of the inquiry of Nellie Barnes of the University of Kansas, into the evolution of stanzaic form, none worth mentioning.   Of the much hoped for Indian poet capable of carrying over the aboriginal lyric impulse into English, there is as yet no arrival indicated.

Until the whole matter of Amerindian melody has been explored and expounded by musicians capable of realizing the creative processes involved, it is impossible to go further in the reëxpression of primitive lyrics.   Of the fifteen lyrics here added to those of the former edition, three are not original collections, but are restated and included because of their relation to the progressions of poetic modes later referred to.   The only apology that can be offered for the rest is that I learned much of primitive poetry in attempting them, and that I discarded more than I included.   There are, however, several interesting conclusions as to the emergence of verse forms other than lyric, which seem as little likely to be disproven as they are certain to overturn several accepted notions of formal sequence. These for the general interest they have, in the renaissance of interest in poetry, are included in this new edition, together with fairly liberal translations.

§ 20

In the Days-of-the-New song was not thought about, but used. It was the authentic notice of something taking place in man's own middle; as authentic as anger, tears or laughter. When the thing that went on in him reached the explosive point, he gave vent to more or less patterned noises, patterned by the path of emotion through his own instrument, a pattern which became rememberable for the relief it afforded. It can never be sufficiently borne in mind that man was in need of frequent relief from the conflict going on within, between his own animality and this strange new factor of manness; his dear and un-familiar animality which he let go even more reluctantly than youth is let go in adolescence, since there was as yet no history nor literature to present manness to him in engaging aspects. What other could he do, then, with this mysterious stranger within himself, entrancing, bedeviling, than try for the conciliations of beauty which are the instinctive accomplishment of song. It is but a short step from the empirical discovery of psychic release by singing, to the notion that song of itself is of magical curative potency. Power over the stranger within being established by singing, power over the stranger without, the Uncreated Spirit of man's invisible environment, was

to the primitive, easily deducible. So man put himself
right with his world by the magic of song, all unaware that
what he sang to was his own under-consciousness. Songs
for health, for skill in hunting and way-finding, for courage
in battle met with affective response. Autonomic centers
were aroused, instincts quickened, rhythmic orchestration
of the whole man produced the condition of well-being in
which man feels equal to his destiny. And this was the
case whether offered singly or communally. Such songs
arose, as Jung puts it, "out of the willed introversion of the
creative mind, retreating before its own problem," and
reached their periphery in the brief reorganization of the
impulses which gave them birth. Thus they remained,
as respects their rhythmic mode, lyrical throughout. There
is no fundamental rhythmic distinction between a man's
"own song" and the song sequences by which tribal
rites are consummated. All such song expression arose
in the complex of humanness and animality which the
Indian describes as his sacred middle, by an impulse toward life-preserving wholeness involving the lyric capacity.
Formal expression so arrived at, remains to this day difficult if not impossible to resolve into its esthetic com-
ponents. Lyric poetry was the last literary mode to be
released from melody, and it is probably not too much to
say that there is no writer of lyrics to-day who would not
add to them the enrichment of music if he could. Yet a
good half of all poetry written is in forms other than lyric.

§ 21

The accepted tradition of the emergence of literary form
has given mnemonics the preference over the lyric im-

pulse, and assumed the prose narrative arising out of easily remembered, poetic measures, gradually ridding itself of melody to establish recitative and a measured but unsung genré of its own. But when unmelodious poetry had been collected and collated in quantity to warrant conclusion, at least so far as Amerind practice is concerned, this did not appear. On the contrary, there was the prose tale, patently gathering to itself rhythm of a sort, measure, not syllabic, but probably based upon mnemonic principles empirically discovered, and the adornments of poetry: assonance, sound sequence, and so far as the genius of the language allowed, metrical pattern. Also, amazingly complete poetic compositions, having no direct relation to lyric impulses and entirely divorced from melodic pattern, were discovered among those tribes for whom narrative was still in the stage of rhythmic elaboration. But for a long time, so generic was the fact to its source, its evolutionary significance remained completely hidden within its own inevitability. After many examples of unsung verse had been collected, responsibility for the subtraction of melody and lyric content appeared to derive from the influence of women; not less securely than the stabilization of the lyric impulse in formal song can be referred to the adventitious working of the male temperament. That lyricism can be fairly classed as a secondary sexual characteristic, but feebly shared by the female, has been formerly a popular way of accounting for the comparative insignificance of the lyric output of women. It should not, however, appear at all astonishing that the more pronounced utilitarianism of women should have turned the lyric invention to social use; to have demanded of it that it should prove itself in being made to "work" more directly than through its affectiveness in raising the plane of male activity.   That poetry can be made to work successfully, to exhibit, as it were, life preservative inherencies, is a group discovery of the utmost ancientness.   And the next important discovery about it was that it worked, in the hands of women, in a direction pointing away from the auto-affectiveness which was its particular function for men.   One concludes, as evidence of the distinction accumulates, that men succeeded best when developing the lyric vein in themselves, and that it was women who put the lyric form as invented by men, to extraneous use. It was perhaps their only important contribution to literary form, but it is deserving of note that its value lies in the variation it points away from the emotional and toward the intellectual use and content of verse. First, and finally, it distinguishes the man's way of handling the universe by trying to get inside it, from the woman's way of manipulating it from the outside.

One begins, in this business of tracing the abstraction of the poetic medium from the lyric mode, with the disposition of the female of whatever species to break down the speech convention of her kind, to a medium simplified for the conveying of assurance of protection to her young. The twitter of hens above the hatch, the mutter of ewes in the lambing pen, the unmistakable warning cry of the quail to her half-hatched brood, the altered sound of every mother sort, advising the farmer that the expected increase of his stock has arrived, the inevitable reversions of human "baby talk," achieving by elisions and doublings and multiplications of syllables, hints of its own earlier forms; this is the root of departure. Here the insistent selfness of the lyric impulse is stripped to no more than the young consciousness can bear; security, reassurance against the shock of life beginning. Tenderness and a little pride perhaps, is the utmost emotional content admitted into mother-song. There must be no wide intervals, no drops and reaches within which the soothing continuity is not well sustained. Melodic pattern and intellectual content exist as the merest excuse for carrying the thread of lyricism reduced to its occasions. No statistical material exists for the determination of relative sense awakenings, whether, for instance, these vary with civilization or the lack of it. I have seen Indian children on their mothers' backs, marking the rhythms of the kiva drums, and taking their place briefly but competently in the dancing line as soon as they are able to walk. But for the appreciation of melody among these same children, three to four years must elapse. Before the ability to "carry a tune" has developed, the natural appetite of the child for verbal rhythms has to be satisfied with verse completely disentangled from anything that could be called song. Thus the poetic mode emerges from its associated modes as pure verbalism, in "nonsense" jingles, in mother-play, and, more than all else, in magic charms.

There is nothing in the function of poetry as magic which, of itself, could have forced the divorcement of words and melody. All song is thought of as to some degree magical in its operation, affective over the beloved, over the cloud and the dew, over the growing corn. Practically all magic of the communal sort is sung: rain songs, hunting songs, songs of mystic seeking. There must have intervened, to insure the elimination of melody, another factor, such as the inability of the child to accomplish melody for himself, or as in the case of the new-born, the advisability of restraining the emotional projection which the melody carries.   In soothing a young infant to sleep passion is not used.   In the singing games of children there is less of melody, less of everything but verbal rhythm, than in the gambling songs of men.   Fundamentally, the inhibitions which governed primitive woman in her earliest and perhaps her only formative contribution to literary modes, are identical with those that later established unsung verse in tribal use.   The chief of these is the failure of social consent.

All the great singing ceremonials, all the dance chorals, Fire dance, Corn dance, War dance, Night Chant of the Navajo, Keres dance of the Emergence, rest upon social consent for the freedom and complexity of their development.   What the people want, the Powers may know.   On the unanimity of wanting and the completeness of expression the fulfillment of the ceremonial depends.   Public good calls for public magic.   But this is not so when the advantage desired is utterly personal and private; when there is not only lack of consent on the part of the subject of the magic song, but active opposition.   For the poem to have power over the attacking enemy, over the reluctant lover, over the particular malevolent spirit, there must be a new mode.   The measure of affectiveness of the uninvited spell, is not altogether in the strength of the wanting, but largely in the degree of resistance to be overcome.   As the inability of the child to be taken with melody, its liability to harm in exposure to intransigent emotion, have to be taken into account in the cradle song; so in the magic formula, the unwittingness of the subject forges the instrument. A spell to be uttered secretly in the dark over the sleeping victim, can not be sung. Nor must the spell which returns the unfaithful lover to his allegiance risk failure through the projection of emotional reactions unfavorable to that end. Under such compulsions the verbal rhythms by which power is to be transmitted, abandon the purely emotional content of the lyric, and take on connotations which must be described as intellectual.

§ 23

When I speak of the intellectual content of primitive magic, I mean no more than that the formulas in question exhibit an acquaintance with the art of suggestion superior to that practised by our own psychologists up to and well along in the past quarter of a century. How such knowledge is adumbrated in the tribal mind is outside the present question. When the Indian of to-day takes on our thought patterns, he does not at the same time acquire a vocabulary for the discussion of nice distinctions in his own. Few Medicine Men can explain more than this of their own practice, that a magic formula "works" better as it is the more poetic; that is to say as it exhibits lyric energy of conception. It works the better for having a "smooth flowing wonder of words"; so that in being recited the mind does not snag in their pronouncement, making openings by which the magic power escapes. A modern practitioner of suggestion would advise that the formula should permit no pauses for lapses of attention; but the explanation of the Medicine Man suffices. Further, in the making of magic spells, for it still goes on, as with us, it is important to exclude everything but the goal of intimate desire. Even as the mother keeps out of her lullaby all color of anxiety or impatience, so the magic maker allows no doubtful or contradictory concept to intrude in the composition of the spell. Finally it is not necessary that the formula be understood. The more intelligent Medicine Men insist that the object of the spell must be understood. When the subject is unaware of the magic being worked against him, then the best formula is that one in which the wish behind it is most explicitly stated. There is a popular preference for unintelligibility in spells which are used on oneself, possibly arising out of the superior values which attach to ancientness, and therefore to formulas likely to contain many archaic or badly remembered words.

There is more than this in the best Amerind formulas obtainable. There is the unconsciously acquired acquaintance with the principle of mnemonics, dictating the break in the repetitive phrases for the reënforcement of attention; the use of sacred numbers. There is the emphasis on the associative values of sounds rather than on their strictly verbal significance. In the affective spell there is ordinarily the invoking of spirits, or deific powers, the dependence of the spell maker on more than himself or the spell, the equivalent of the auto-evocation of our once popular Coué.

In the merely protective or prophylactic formulas, such as are passed about in common exchange, like a favorite prescription for what to do when you feel a cold coming on, invocation and lyric energy are generally lacking.

These are reserved for the spell which is preciously communicated under appropriate professional safeguards. In the best, and latest, of the Amerind formulas collated from various collections, there is that careful placing of the picture of the wish, which is not found outside of the culture called primitive, until it appears among the great masters of Christian magic, notably in the recommended spiritual exercises of the Ignatian mystics. The two modes which can be found current in poetic magic of the Stone Age, are amply illustrated in the Cherokee formulas collected by James Mooney, in one of which the picture centers upon the person of the Wisher, and in the other is built up of pure observation about the Wish. These constitute the earliest formalized departure from the provocative incompleteness of the Indian lyric. One suspects that the influence of these things on poetic form can be traced much further than the Stone Age in which they originated.

§ 24

Early, so early in this study that I did not know what I had found, Tinnemahá of the Owens Valley Paiutes, consented to recite for me the whole cycle of twin brother tales, Hínunö and Pamaquásh, the right and left hands of Sun Power, the down pull and the up pull of Universal force. He was to recite it for me after the fashion of the Ancients, of which he was almost the sole inheritor in his campody. It was to be done of early winter evenings when no snakes were about, and the Twins themselves were quiescent. There went an unspecified amount of ceremonial preparation to the event, which I was to understand would be otherwise attended with considerable peril, and a supper for which the hearer paid. There was ceremonial smoke, and aromatic herbs burnt on the little fire and low, around which we sat with our backs to the Wickiup wall. There was music; not a song. It had no words nor any tune. It had time, which was clicked out by the singing elders with willow wands, in one end of which a wedge-shaped split had been made for a matter of a foot or two. Properly handled, they produced a sound like the smooth continuous rattle of castanets, but softer, and beautifully synchronized. To this accompaniment the music wandered, a thread of unpatterned melody, unpatterned as blowing wind or flowing water. So far as I was able to discover, with divided attention, throughout the long evening the music returned not once to any phrase, nor any repetitious sequence of intervals. It had no effect of being rehearsed; one of the two voices seemed occasionally the least fraction of a tone in advance, unobtrusively caught up by the other. At any given moment it seemed always about to develop into explicit melody and never did. It poured, an ever so slightly muted stream of vocalization submitting to labial and aspirated modifications, but never to one closed consonant, with never a break, except such as was in response to breaks in the narrative, and with never an instant's hesitation. And under it went the steady, unaccented Pyrrhic rhythm of the split wands. Over it, the narrative rode like a bird on running water, now carried by it, now putting its wings down for a firm forward stroke, equally unpatterned in movement, but never in direct opposition to the singing sound. In the spoken tale there was neither meter nor stanza nor tonal variation other than is natural to narrative speech. This, said Tinnemahá, was how it was done in the time of our Ancients.

A singular and engaging instance; too singular to prove anything! Years afterward I heard the same sort of thing among the Utes, heard of it among the Papagoes; and after other years, rediscovered it among the Rio Grande Pueblos.[13] Finally Frances Dinsmore recorded such an unpatterned Ute melody, possibly the one I heard, which she described as accompanying a legendary narrative. She called the vocalization "not a song, but the stuff from which songs are made." Was the accompanying narrative the stuff from which poetry that is not lyric is made? Is it perhaps the "polyphonic prose" which Miss Lowell found lurking in a dim, ancestral corner of her mind, and brought forward as a new discovery?

There is need of some such primary invention to account for the tribal lay. Narrative poetry can not be deduced out of the lyric sequence which carries the ceremonial rite. In the myth which informs Amerind ceremonial dance-drama, the choruses, sung and danced, are projected from the high moments of the story. The intervening narrative events are carried in ritualistic, symbolic acts; the story of them is always present in the tribal mind, as the original plots of Greek drama were present with the audience; told as fireside tales, or, when of esoteric value, communicated by initiation. The normal evolution of a myth so celebrated is toward drama, as the Greek myths traveled, by the introduction of dialogue and the objectifying of incidents at first only symbolized. Among the Keres, the Hopi, and at Zuñi this process of dramatization may be seen following the Greek progressions as they have come down to us. The mode remains lryic throughout; the rhythms are the rhythms of the environment to which tribal man assimilates himself in this fashion, modified by their own emotional evocation.

§ 25

We are put at fault in our prepossessions about literary origins by the manner in which the primitive tale is communicated to us.   Collectors of tribal literature in the original, testify generally to their rhythmic mode; but in the bald transliterations of the ethnologist, or the crabbed English vocabulary of the Government School trained native, their æsthetic values are overwhelmingly depressed. As they came forth normally, the prose rhythms of folk narrative are as distinct as their speech idioms.   In all of them there is a basic rhythm of perceptivity, the mind of the story-teller working on his plot with the movement of deglutition, onset and relaxation, rippling like the swallowing muscles of the snake.   In this connection it is to be recalled that the perception of story, the ability to recall in their true order causal sequences in behavior, is one of the distinctions which brought man down out of the trees as something other than ape.   So far no evidence has been offered that the ape [14] kind can tell themselves stories; only the dog kind, the elephant and man can do just that for themselves.   Man goes further and tells himself stories that mean something other than appears in the described events.   Overtones of the intellectual process involved still color the progressions of these earlier tales, inhibiting, for the occasion of the telling, all involved emo-

tions.   If, as Tinnemahá insisted, our ancients told their
stories to the running accompaniment of unpatterned
music, it might very well be that the music enabled the
teller to hold himself to the uninterrupted level of narra-
tion.   It might have been, in the Days-of-the-New, a way
of ridding the story-maker of the emotional burden—
putting it aside into the flute, the harp, the lyre—leaving
him the freer for the firm, indispensable hold on the story's
thread.

§ 26

Immeasurable more work must be done in this field
before the evolutionary sequence comes clear.   The next
contribution to narrative verse, though with what unre-
covered lapses between is but to be guessed, was in the
direction of rememberability.   It began with the Sayings
of the Ancient Men, which are in general the myths behind
the rites by which individuals are initiated into tribal
mysteries.   Here the need is of exactness in transmission
and authentication.   The word has power, but it must be
the veritable word of the fathers: "they say;" "it has been
said;" "verily, it has been said, at this time, in this house."
These are the tags of authentic tradition, which turned
up later as Thus sayeth the Lord of holy scriptures.   In
between, the communicated wisdom is arranged primarily
so to be easily remembered, all the more easily because
appealing to the æsthetic sense through provocative
phrasing, pleasing sound sequences, rhythms of familiarity.

There is wide variation in the literary composition of
the Sayings, which in their exact forms are known perhaps
only to the heads of the religious societies to which they

pertain.   Probably as an aid to easy retention—for they
are often long, and repetitious to a tedious degree—they
tend to be recited in a sing-song, or rise occasionally to a
chant.   The primitive mind, however, unexhausted by
the multiplicity of sensations which beset the modern
attention, can respond again and again to the same stroke,
with undiminished freshness of enjoyment.   In many of
the tribal lays in which catalogues of creation, lists of par-
ticipants, instances of humorous or mystical revelation,
are called for, or are on any ground admissible to the tale,
one sees the widening rings of recognition on the part of
the audience, dying only when response has been stretched
far beyond what the sophisticated attention can bear.
The catalogue of ships in the Iliad, for which most modern
translators feel it obligatory to apologize, was probably
included out of an older version of the heroic lays, because
of the pleasure it gave the more primitive majority of the
audience.   It is the same sort of pleasure provided the
child mind in the song of Noah and his Ark, with the
animals going in two by two.

Every possible variation of tribal lays on their way to
be gathered into the tribal epic, may be collected here at
home, exhibiting every intellectual trick experimentally
acquired in the lyric and the magic formula: rhythm pattern, sound sequence, incremental thought rhythm, rhythmic clusters, cadenced phrasing—but never to my knowledge metrical rhythm as modernly applied.   For poetic
quality one has to depend on fresh rhythmic perception,
and flashes of observation at once more lyrical and more
acute than happens with us, except in the rare instances of
genius . . . the great snake "making a sound as of blowing

of wind," the beaver describing the gods making way for him as the parting of waters in the forked ripple-spread of his swimming.

Of the final adumbration of intellectual technique and lyric perception into the tribal epic, there is still too much unstudied to warrant conclusion. That epics of creation, of tribal myth and history, do exist among our own Indians, equal in intellectual sweep, in poetic content and literary technique—superior occasionally—to anything produced by the primitive races of Europe, is so well known that a certain shame attaches to any reference to them which does not also convey the assurance that they are being meticulously preserved and intelligently studied. Unhappily the literary scholarship of the United States hangs out its tongue with eagerness while it paws the scrap heap of Europe for smeared mythological reference or misplaced dative cases, under a Government policy which grandiosely announces the conversion of the makers and cherishers of our native epics into three dollar a day laborers.

At Zuñi the noblest version of creation—truer to the event as it is apprehended by modern science than the account in Genesis—has been recorded and for proof partly translated. It is known to not more than two or three of our poets and to none of the heads of Departments of literature. At Taos, where the epic whole is divided in two parts each requiring two hours for recital, it is preciously and precariously preserved by the priests of the sacred societies. In the Keres pueblos the sacred epic is so guarded from White spoliation that it is likely to be finally extinguished with the lives of the jealous elders who dare not submit it to youth trained in the brash and stupid ignorance of the Government schools.[15]

It is from Mexico probably that the answers to unsolved problems of literary origins will come in completeness. There scholarship is less pretentious, less thumb-printed by tradition. There the rhythms of intellectualism are genetic to the rhythms of creative impulses, rhythms of the land, the life, the racial inheritance, without being any the less American. In the meantime, there is this contribution.

Amerindian Songs

Reëxpressed from the Originals

by

Mary Austin

HEART'S FRIEND

Fair is the white star of twilight
And the sky clearer
At the day's end;
But she is fairer,
And she is dearer,
She, my heart's friend!

Fair is the white star of twilight
And the moon roving
To the sky's end;
But she is fairer,
And she is dearer,
She, my heart's friend!

From the Paiute.

THE GRASS ON THE MOUNTAIN

Oh, long, long
The snow has possessed the mountains.

The deer have come down and the big-horn,
They have followed the Sun to the south
To feed on the mesquite pods and the bunch grass.
Loud are the thunder drums
In the tents of the mountains.

Oh, long, long
Have we eaten *chia* seeds
And dried deer's flesh of the summer killing.
We are wearied of our huts
And the smoky smell of our garments.

We are sick with desire of the sun
And the grass on the mountain.

From the Paiute.

SONG FOR THE PASSING OF A BEAUTIFUL WOMAN

Strong sun across the sod can make
Such quickening as your countenance!

I am more worth for what your passing wakes,
Great races in my loins, to you that cry.
My blood is redder for your loveliness.

From the Paiute.

SONG FOR THE NEWBORN

To be sung by the one who first takes the child from its mother.

Newborn, on the naked sand
Nakedly lay it.
Next to the earth mother,
That it may know her;
Having good thoughts of her, the food giver.

Newborn, we tenderly
In our arms take it,
Making good thoughts.
House-god, be entreated,
That it may grow from childhood to manhood,
Happy, contented;
Beautifully walking
The trail to old age.
Having good thoughts of the earth its mother,
That she may give it the fruits of her being.
Newborn, on the naked sand
Nakedly lay it.

Grande Pueblos.

WARRIOR'S SONG

Weep not for me, Loved Woman,
Should I die;
But for yourself be weeping!

Weep not for warriors who go
Gladly to battle.
Theirs to revenge
Fallen and slain of our people;
Theirs to lay low
All our foes like them,
Death to make, singing.

Weep not for warriors,
But weep for women!
Oh, weep for all women!

Theirs to be pitied
Most of all creatures,
Whose men return not!
How shall their hearts be stayed
When we are fallen?

Weep not for me, Loved Woman,
For yourself alone be weeping!

THE EAGLE'S SONG

Said the Eagle:
  I was astonished
  When I heard that there was death.

  My home, alas,
  Must I leave it!
  All beholding summits,
  Shall I see thee no more!

  North I went,
  Leaning on the wind;
  Through the forest resounded
  The cry of the hunted doe.

  East I went,
  Through the hot dawning;
  There was the smell of death in my nostrils.

  South I went, seeking
  The place where there is no death.
  Weeping I heard
  The voice of women
  Wailing for their children.

  West I went,
  On the world encompassing water;
  Death's trail was before me.

People, O people,
Needs be that we must die!

Therefore let us make
Songs together.
With a twine of songs to bind us
To the middle Heaven,
The white way of souls.
There we shall be at rest,
With our songs
We shall roam no more!

Southern California.

YOUNG MEN'S SONG

Ah—ahou! Ahou—aou! *
Hi! Hi! Hi! Hi-ah-ee—ah!

Go we now,
    Go we now,
        Go . . o . . o now!
Ahou! Ahou! Ahou! Ahou!

Go we where the trail leads,
    It leads before us!

Ahou . . aou . . aou . . aou . . aou . . aou! †
Ai . . ai . . ai . . ai . . ai . . ai!
Go we
    Go we
        Go . . o . . o now!
Many scalps
We shall bring returning.

Go we
    Ahou!
        Ahou!
Hi! Hi! Hi!
Ai . . ai . . ai . . ai . . ai . . ai . . i . . ee!

* Call to attract the attention of War god.
† Prolong by clapping hand on mouth.

94

WOMAN'S SONG

These are the First Born
Of the First People.
Topal, the grinding stone,
Kenhut, the wampum string,
Paviut, the knife.

When the Empty Quietness
Begot the Engendering Mist,
Then came the Sky Man,
Came the Earth Mother,
Who made the Grinding Stone,
Who made the Hunting Knife,
Who made the Wampum String.

Thus runs the song around,
Under what tribal change soe'er you find them.
Where there are women found
There sits the grinding stone;
Where there are men
There glints the hunting knife;
Where there are People
There goes the wampum string.
Thus runs the song around.

From the Luiseño.

A SONG IN DEPRESSION

Now all my singing dreams are gone!
None knows where they have fled
Nor by what trails they have left me.

Return, O dreams of my heart,
And sing in the summer twilight,
By the creek and the almond thicket
And the field that is bordered with lupines.

Now is my refuge to seek
In the hollow of friendly shoulders,
Since the singing is stopped in my pulse
And the earth and the sky refuse me.
Now must I hold by the eyes of a friend
When the high white stars are unfriendly.

Over sweet is the refuge for trusting.
Return and sing, O my Dreams,
In the dewy and palpitant pastures,
Till the love of living awakes
And the strength of the hills to uphold me!

From the Washoe-Paiute.

SIOUX SONG AT PARTING

Breaks now, breaks now my heart,
Thinking, from thee I part.
Hear thou what says my heart:
Keep me,
Keep me in thine alway!

Dreams now, dreams now my heart.
Weeping, awake I start,
Thinking, again we part.
Dream thou,
Perchance thy dream will stay!

THE YIELDING HEART

Too soon I yield, I fear,
Too soon!
Yet yielding I rejoice
That in your touch
Such power should be,
Such magic in your voice!

From the Yokut.

COME NOT NEAR MY SONGS

Come not near my songs,
You who are not my lover,
Lest from out that ambush
Leaps my heart upon you!

When my songs are glowing
As an almond thicket
With the bloom upon it,
Lies my heart in ambush
All amid my singing;
Come not near my songs,
You who are not my lover!

Do not hear my songs,
You who are not my lover!
Over-sweet the heart is,
Where my love has bruised it,
Breathe you not that fragrance,
You who are not my lover.
Do not stoop above my song,
With its languor on you,
Lest from out my singing
Leaps my heart upon you!

From the Shoshone.

SONG OF THE BASKET DANCERS

I

We, the Rain Cloud callers,
Ancient mothers of the Rain Cloud clan,
Basket bearers;
We entreat you,
O ye Ancients,
By the full-shaped womb,
That the lightning and the thunder and the rain
Shall come upon the earth,
Shall fructify the earth;
That the great rain clouds shall come upon the earth
As the lover to the maid.

II

Send your breath to blow the clouds,
O ye Ancients,
As the wind blows the plumes
Of our eagle-feathered prayer sticks,
Send, O ye Ancients,
To the Six Corn Maidens.
To the White Corn Maiden,
To the Yellow Corn Maiden,
To the Red Corn Maiden,

To the Blue Corn Maiden,
To the Many Colored Maiden,
To the Black Corn Maiden,
That their wombs bear fruit.

III

Let the thunder be heard,
O ye Ancients!
Let the sky be covered with white blossom clouds,
That the earth, O ye Ancients,
Be covered with many colored flowers.
That the seeds come up,
That the stalks grow strong
That the people have corn,
That happily they eat.
Let the people have corn to complete the road of life.

LAMENT OF A MAN FOR HIS SON

Son, my son!

I will go up to the mountain
And there I will light a fire
To the feet of my son's spirit,
And there will I lament him;
Saying,
O my son,
What is my life to me, now you are departed!

Son, my son,
In the deep earth
We softly laid thee in a Chief's robe,
In a warrior's gear.
Surely there,
In the spirit land
Thy deeds attend thee!
Surely,
The corn comes to the ear again!

But I, here,
I am the stalk that the seed-gatherers
Descrying empty, afar, left standing.
Son, my son!
What is my life to me, now you are departed?

MEDICINE SONGS

These are the songs of the Friend,
Made by the Medicine Man
In the young dusk of the Spring, moonless and tender.

At the hour when balm-giving herbs
Begin to be musky and sweet along the creek border,
When the smell of the sage is sharp in the trail of the
  cattle,
And the ants run busily still up the boles of the pine
  trees,
I heard the pound of his feet, and the roll of his ram's
  horn rattle.
Sweet was the drone of his song,
And the night desirous.

All night he sang,
Till the young, thin moon came up,
About the wolf hour of the morning.

The eyes of the Medicine Man
Were pale as the sloughs at sun-dawn.
The shadow of all his songs
Strewed the cheek hollows
Like ash in the pits of the hearthstone,
Bitter and thick was his voice
With the dust stirred up by his dancing.

These are the songs he made
To be sung for endurance of friendship,
Which still in my heart I hear
When I go by the sweet-smelling trails
In the moonless evenings of April.
My pulse is full of their whisper and beat,
Overfull and aching with song
And the roll of the ram's horn rattle,
When the smell of the camphire comes out by the creeks,
And the nights are young and desirous.

FIRST SONG

O winding trails that run out every way
To seek the happy places of the hills,
And stars that swirl about the hollow heaven,
You hear the rising of my songs
Like a morning full of wings.

O little trails, that whiten through the dunes,
A light is on you more than day has made.
And all my mind goes from me like a flame
To couple with the live thought of the world,
Because of this my friend.

SECOND SONG

What is this that stirs beside me
What sweet troubling?

It is my thought that quickens to my friend.
For my thought was as a woman
When her time is past and she bears no children.
Now the time returns
Tremulous and quick as my friend goes by me.

Now is my walking changed
And my strength braced with laughter.
I am so much more to myself
As the friend of my friend,
That the days shall not affront me,
Nor sighs, little sisters of pain, come nigh me.

THIRD SONG

Good is a maid in the hut
In the undark nights in summer
When her sides are slim and brown
And you prove her by her laughter.
But the love of man to man
Has mighty works to prove it.

FOURTH SONG

Lo, my heart is as a lair.
It is hidden under my songs,
And my dancing is a screen before its ways.

There my friend shall keep darkly,
When ill repute pursues him
There he shall lie safe
From malice and dishonor.

PAPAGO LOVE SONGS

I

Early I rose
In the blue morning;
My love was up before me,
It came running to me from the doorways of the Dawn.

On Papago Mountain
The dying quarry
Looked at me with my love's eyes.

II

Do you long, my Maiden,
For bisnaga blossoms
To fasten in your hair?

I will pick them for you.
What are bisnaga spines to me
Whom love is forever pricking in the side?

GLYPHS

I

A girl wearing a green ribbon,—
As if it had been my girl.
—The green ribbon I gave her for remembrance—
Knowing all the time it was not my girl,
Such was the magic of that ribbon,
Suddenly,
My girl existed inside me!

II

Your face is strange,
And the smell of your garments,
But your soul is familiar;
As if in dreams our thoughts
Had visited one another.

Often from unremembering sleep
I wake delicately glowing.
Now I know what my heart has been doing.

Now I know why when we met
It slipped
So easily into loving.

III

Truly buzzards
Around my sky are circling!

For my soul festers,
And an odor of corruption
Betrays me to disaster.

Meanness, betrayal and spite
Come flockwise,
To make me aware
Of sickness and death within me.
My sky is full of the dreadful sound
Of the wings of unsuccesses.

From the Washoe-Paiute.

NEITHER SPIRIT NOR BIRD

Neither spirit nor bird;
That was my flute you heard
Last night by the river.
When you came with your wicker jar
Where the river drags the willows,
That was my flute you heard,
Wacoba, Wacoba,
Calling, Come to the willows!

Neither the wind nor a bird
Rustled the lupine blooms.
That was my blood you heard
Answer your garment's hem
Whispering through the grasses;
That was my blood you heard
By the wild rose under the willows.

That was no beast that stirred,
That was my heart you heard,
Pacing to and fro
In the ambush of my desire,
To the music my flute let fall.
Wacoba, Wacoba,
That was my heart you heard
Leaping under the willows.

From the Shoshone.

RAIN SONGS FROM THE RIO GRANDE
PUEBLOS

I

People of the middle heaven
Moving happily behind white floating cloud masks,
Moving busily behind rain-straitened cloud masks;
People of the Lightning,
People of the Thunder,
People of the Rainbow,
Rain! Rain! Rain!

II

Cloud priests,
Whose hearts ascend through the spruce tree
On the Mountains of the North,
   Pray for us!
Cloud priests,
Whose hearts ascend
Through the pine of the West,
Through the oak of the South,
Through the aspen of the East,
Through the high-branched cedar of the zenith,
Through the low, dark cedar of the nadir,
   Pray for us!

III

Archpriests of the six world quarters,
         Work with us!
That the waters of the six great springs of the world
May fructify the Earth, our mother,
That she bring forth fruit for us!

We, the ancient ones,
From the four womb-worlds,
From the doorway of the underworld,
From Shipapu,
We, assembling,
Lifting up our thoughts to the clouds,
To the lightning, to the thunder,
Lifting up our hearts,
Make you precious medicine.

People of the Middle World,
Send your thoughts to us!
That our songs go straightly
On the sacred meal road,
The ancient road,
Walking it with power.
Send your thoughts to us!

Send to the cloud priests,
Send to the archpriests;
That their songs may bring the waters
To fructify the Earth;
That the Sun embrace the Earth
That she bring forth fruit.

IV

People of the lightning,
Send your serpent darting arrows!
Hear the thunder beating
With its wings of dark cloud!

Who is this that cometh?
People of the trees on the six world mountains,
Standing up to pray for rain,
All your people and your thoughts
   Come to us!

Who is this that cometh?
   People of the dark cloud,
   Let your thoughts come to us!
People of the lightning,
   Let your thoughts come to us!
People of the blue-cloud horizon,
   Let your thoughts come to us!
Rain! Rain! Rain!

A SONG OF GREATNESS [16]

When I hear the old men,
Telling of heroes,
Telling of great deeds of ancient days,
When I hear that telling,
Then I think within me
I, too, am one of these.

When I hear the tribesmen
Praising great ones,
Praising warriors of ancient days,
When I hear that praising
Then I know that I, too,
Shall be esteemed,
I, too, when my time comes,
Shall do mightily.

Sioux?

PERSONAL SONG OF RED FOX

On that stone ridge I go,
   Hauh, hauh!
East I go,
   Hauh, hauh!
On the white road I go
Crouching I go,
   Hauh, hauh!
I yelp on the road of stars.
   Hauh, hauh.

Northern California.

SONG OF A WOMAN ABANDONED BY THE TRIBE BECAUSE SHE IS TOO OLD TO KEEP UP WITH THEIR MIGRATION [17]

Alas, that I should die,
That I should die now,
I who know so much!

It will miss me,
The twirling fire stick;
The fire coal between the hearth stones,
It will miss me.

The Medicine songs,
The songs of magic healing;
The medicine herbs by the water borders,
They will miss me;
The basket willow,
It will miss me;
All the wisdom of women,
It will miss me.

Alas, that I should die,
Who know so much.

Southern Shoshone.

PERSONAL SONG OF DANIEL RED EAGLE [18]

The fierce hawk of death is over me,
The fierce hawk of death.

Now and again
Its wing shadows
Brush my shoulders.

The fierce hawk of death,
When will it strike!

Oglalla Sioux.

SONG OF SEEKING [19]

The dear of my soul
I have lost it;
That lost Other
I am seeking;
All night awake
I am seeking.
I shall leave no place unsearched till I find her.
At day break,
I seemed to see her,
It was only
The flash of a loon's wing on the water,
It is not that Other whom my soul seeketh.

Chippewa.

THUNDER DANCE AT SAN ILDEFONSO [20]

I

We are calling on the dark cloud
Calling on the dun cloud,
On the eagle-feathered clouds
From their mountain eyries.
Come, clouds, come
And bring the summer rain.

II

Hear the thunder calling
With the voice of many villages,
With the sound of hollow drums,
With the roll of pebbled gourds
Like the swish of rushing rain.
Hoonah, hoonah,
The voice of the thunder
Calling on the clouds to bring the summer rain.

III

Slow   cloud
Low   cloud
Wing-hovering cloud
Over the thirsty fields,
Over the waiting towns
Low   cloud,   slow   cloud
Let the rain down!

Over the blossoming beans
Over the tasseling corn.
All day over the thirsty fields
Let the rain down!

Tewa.

CRADLE SONG

Coo . . . ah . . . coo . . . !
Little Dove,
Coo . . ah . . coo!

The wind is rocking
Thy nest in the pine bough,
My arms are rocking
Thy nest, little Dove.

Coo . . . ah . . . . coo
Little Dove
Sleep Little Dove
Coo . . oo . oooo Little Dove!

Paiute.

GAMBLING SONG

OFTEN SUNG AS A LULLABY

Glossy Locks, picks them up,
Picks them up, picks them up.

Red Moccasin picks them up,
Picks them up,
The Winning ones,
The Lucky ones,
Glossy Locks picks them up
My little Dove!

Navajo.

TWO SONGS OF VICTORY [21]

COMMEMORATIVE SONG AND DANCE OF
PIAUTES FOR A VICTORY OVER THE MOJAVE

Hey-yah, hey-yah, hey
Ha . aha . ha-ha

(The dancers circle the fire holding bows in position
for stooping shots.)

This is what we do,
This is what we do,
This is what we do to our enemies.

(They leap, as over dead bodies stretched on the
ground.)

Hah!
The feast is spread,
Come to the feast,
Come you to the feast
O ye vultures,
On wide wings soaring,
Come to the feast,
O ye vultures!

(Dancers balance their arms like wings, and leap over
the swelling bodies.)

Hey-yah, hey-yah, hey,
Ha, aha, ha-ha,
This is the feast we have spread.

VICTORY SONG OF THE FOX

I

I am the one that was blessed,
I am the one.
The sharp arrows of our enemies,
From me they turned aside.
I am the one whose body
Was made holy.

II

They begin to whet their beaks,
Those sacred ones,
Those hungry ones.
They whet their forked beaks
They begin to open their mouths
In the middle of the sky,
Those hungry ones.
They move their beaks, assembling.

SONG OF A MAN WHOSE FATHER WAS KILLED IN WAR

Something red my father wears now,
Where his life was.

O young men,
Whose wound stripes are on your sleeves
Walk you reverently
Pronouncing my father's name.

O my father,
I hear the old men saying
There goes a warrior's son.

Sioux.

SONG OF A MAN ABOUT TO DIE IN A
STRANGE LAND

If I die here
In a strange land,
If I die
In a land not my own,
Nevertheless, the thunder
The rolling thunder
Will take me home.

If I die here, the wind,
The wind rushing over the prairie
The wind will take me home.

The wind and the thunder,
They are the same everywhere,
What does it matter, then,
If I die here in a strange land?

Ojibway.

PILGRIMAGE SONG

That mountain there,
That white-shell mountain,
Toward the east it standeth,
O sacred mountain,
Whence the day springs.
O white-shell mountain,
Guard thou our day!

Yonder, afar,
That dark blue mountain,
Toward the north standing
That sacred mountain,
Whence the storm cometh,
O dark blue mountain,
Spare not our storm!

That mountain there,
That turquoise-colored mountain,
Toward the west it standeth,
The path of life unending
And beyond it,
O turquoise mountain,
Guide thou our way!

Yonder, afar,
Rose-yellow mountain,

Sacred southern mountain,
Yonder afar, in beauty walking,
The way of joy unending;
Rose-yellow mountain,
Keep thou our home!

EARTH SONG [22]

Into the earth my grandfathers dug,
In the palms of their hands they gathered its soil,
In the palms of their hands they gathered its soil,
Into the earth my grandfathers dug,
In the palms of their hands they moistened its soil.
In the palms of their hands they rubbed its soil.

Into the earth my grandfathers dug
The Sacred One, the Ancient One,
Into the earth they dug.
Upon their faces they placed its soil
Upon their foreheads they placed its soil.

Behold it upon my forehead,
The symbol my grandfathers made.
That which I gathered in the hollow of my hand
I put it upon my face and my forehead,
The symbol of the Sacred One, the Ancient One,
The soil of the earth my grandfathers dug,
I put it upon my forehead.

Osage

STAR SONG [23]

We are the singing stars,
We sing with our light.
We are the birds of fire,
Through the heavens we take our flight.

Our light is as a star,
Making a road for spirits.

Among us are three hunters
Forever chasing a bear.
There never was a time
When they three were not hunting.

We look down upon the mountains.

Passamaquoddy.

Magic Formulas from the Cherokee [24]

FORMULA FOR SECURING AFFECTION

Hearken!

In Alahiyi, O Terrible Woman,   hear me!
In Alahiyi, where your rest is, O White-Fire Woman, you
    have drawn close to hear me.

Most Beautiful!   Being with you, none are ever lonely.
Instantly, being with you, I also am rendered fireful.
So that none with me shall ever be lonely!

Now you have emblazoned the path of my life,
It shall never be dreary.
You have put my feet in the White way, with no shadow of
    blueness.
You have put my feet in the flame's way,
It shall never be desolate;
You have brought down for me the White way of souls.
There in the midst of earth horizon you have placed me.
I shall stand erect upon the earth
And no one who is with me shall ever be desolate.
Behold, I am comely!
You have put me into the White house, the aura of all
    things desirable!
It moves with me as I move in the midst of it,
And no one with me shall ever know desolation of spirit.
Truly, White-Fire Woman, by your power

You have caused it to be so with me
That I shall never be disconsolate.

Truly, from Alahiyi, you have shadowed the soul of the
woman of my desire.
Now the path of her life you have made dreary.
Let her be completely veiled in loneliness.
Set her feet in the blue road;
Bring her soul down to the low places of the earth;
Where her feet are now, wherever she stands let desolation
leave its mark upon her.
That she may turn to me; that she may seek warmth of me;
Where she stands let her be marked out for loneliness.

Hah! Woman of my desire!
I belong to the Wolf Clan, that clan which was allotted to
you from the beginning.
No one with me is ever lonely in spirit,
For I am in the flame's way.   I am well-looking.
Let her put her soul in the center of my soul never to turn
away.
In the midst of other men, grant that she shall never think
of them.

O desirable woman,
I am of the one clan which was destined for you when the
Seven Clans were established.

Where other men are there is no aura of happiness.
They are loathly to you.

The polecat has made them like himself; they are fit only
for his company.
They are utterly inconsiderable!

The common possum has made them like himself; they are
fit only for his company:
Turn wholly from them.

The hoarse rain-crow has made them so like himself; they
are fit only for his company:
They are altogether loathsome.

All the seven clans alike are desolating to the spirit.
They have no comeliness,
They are clothed with the leavings of the tribe,
They go about covered with filth.
But I . . . I am ordained to be kin to the fire-flame,
I am white-burning;
I stand with my face to the Sun-Land,
I shall never be desolate!
Behold, how handsome I am,
Wherever I go I am covered with the everlasting aura of
whiteness,
No one with me shall ever be lonely of spirit.

Your soul has come into the very center of my soul never to
turn away.
I take your soul.

Hearken!

FORMULA FOR SEPARATING LOVERS

Ah, you dweller of the high places,
Blue Hawk, trouble bringer, of the far distant lake,
The blue smoke of tobacco I offer you in recompense!

Ah, now you have arisen;
At once you have come down to me;
You have alighted mid-way between them,
Those two that I have named to you;
At once their souls you have bemused,
At once they have become separated.

I am a man whose soul is white-glowing,
I stand at the sunrise; in me
The fire-sperm shall be proof against desolation of spirit.

This woman is of the Paint Clan, she is called Wayi.
Instantly we shall turn her soul about,
Instantly it shall be accomplished.

We shall turn it about as we go toward the Sun-land.
I am a man who abides in the aura of happiness;
Here where I establish it, her soul shall come close against
        mine,
Let her eyes be ever turning to me and watching,
Where my body is there shall be for her no loneliness.

136

FORMULA FOR FIXING AFFECTION

(The following is recited at night, by stealth, whisperingly,
over the person whose affections it is desired to secure.)

Yuh! Hah!

Now the souls have come together.
You are of the Deer Clan,
Your name is Ayasta.
I am of the Deer Clan.

(One of the following is recited four times on each one of
four consecutive nights.)

FIRST NIGHT
Your body I take, the whole of you.
I absorb it into myself.

SECOND NIGHT
Your flesh I take, the form of you.
I absorb it into myself.

THIRD NIGHT
Your essence I take, the soul of you.
I absorb it into myself.

FOURTH NIGHT
Your heart I take, the affections of you,
I absorb them into myself.

137

(After each recitation of the above the hands of the performer are held toward the fire and a little ashes, preferably mixed with spittle of the performer, are rubbed gently on the breast of the subject.)

Hearken!   Hah!

Now our souls have met, never to part.
You have declared it, O Ancient One Above,
O Black Spider, you have been drawn down from on high,
You have let down your web.

She is of the Deer Clan,
Her name is Ayasta.
You have enmeshed her soul in your web.
You have caused her to know
That where the people of the Seven Clans are coming
    and going,
There is never any feeling of loneliness,
Never any desolation of spirit.

Hearken!   Hah!

You have covered her over with loneliness;
Her eyes have faded from all she looked upon,
Her eyes have come to fasten on me alone.
Whither can her soul escape!

Let her be sorrowing where she goes,
And not for one night only;
Let her spirit go aimlessly wandering

On a trail that can never be followed.
Never by any soul but my soul.
O Black Spider you hold her in your web,
Never shall she break through its meshes.
What is the name of the soul,
Now they two have come together?
Her soul, it is mine,
They shall never be separated.

Hearken! Hah!

Now you have given heed to me, O Ancient Red-Fire.
O terrible one, dweller in the heart-coal,
Your grandchildren come to the edge of your abiding
    place,
To the fire's edge holding out our hands to you.
You hold them yet more firmly, never to let go your grasp.
O Ancient One, Red-Fire, we two have become one.
The woman has put her soul into our hands.
We shall never let go.
It is accomplished.
Yuh!

FORMULA FOR TURNING ASIDE A STORM

Here you come, He-wind,
In your rutting wrath
Trampling and tossing.
Truly, I fear you!
But it is not I you are tracking.
It is your mate, whose footprints
Flash in white riffles of leaves
Up the slope of the mountain.

Follow where I point you,
Where she goes through the tops of the trees,
Where your path leads,
There in the middle air
None shall disturb your mating.
Let your path go
Where the wavy branches meet
On the lofty mountain!

Tribal Lays

HÍ–NU–NO AND PA–MA–QUÁSH

THE FINAL ADVENTURE OF THE TWIN BROTHERS OF THE
OWENS VALLEY PAIUTES

This is a Telling of our Fathers' fathers, how when they
Twain had accomplished the whole of their adventures,
Hí-nu-no was greatly vexed with his older brother, for
so it was that when anything was broken or destroyed
by Hí-nu-no, Pa-ma-quásh would mend and remake it;
he made it to be as if it had never been broken.   Thus
he had done with the cubs of the bear that Hí-nu-no
had swung on the tops of the bended pine trees.   Thus
with the digging sticks of the women of Säg-ha-ra-
wí-te.

Thus it was said by our Fathers' fathers, how of they Twain
Hí-nu-no, the younger, was greatly angered, saying:
Behold how my elder brother makes me to be as nothing at all, utterly insignificant, so that the people laugh
and the things that I do become of no effect whatever.

Thus in the days of the old, it has been said by our fathers,
that Hí-nu-no the younger thought in his heart and
considered how he would do by himself that which his
brother would not be able to mend; and the mark of this
thing that he did should remain a remembrance of the
anger of Hí-nu-no against Pa-ma-quásh his elder
brother.   So said our Fathers.

Thus, in vexation, Hí-nu-no went apart in the desert places
to dance the dance of his anger and grievous vexation

of spirit.   Four days he danced it, and as his power in-
creased through the fury of dancing, Hí-nu-no became,
through the power of his magic, wide like a wind and
mighty as a wind of the desert places, such as lift up
the face of the desert and carry it on their wings, filling
the hollow sky with the sand and the sound of anger.

This was the way of they Twain, that they became as they
would, and made of the wind and the cloud their bodies, for the fulfillment of urgent wanting.   Through the
forest went Hí-nu-no as the wind of burning, laying
the trees in rows like marsh grass cut for thatching,
splintering the huge trees like willows that the women
strip with their teeth for basket making.   Through the
forest he went like a stag in rut through the brush on
the mountain.   He gathered the hills in his hands, he
scooped hollows, he scattered the hills over the level
places.   The black rock he scattered like gambling
pieces, the red rock like chaff that is winnowed.

This was how he did in the place that is called Lost Borders,
where the borders of the tribes run out, and the wild
sheep find no pasture.   He loosened his flint from his
belt, the flint knife for skinning and fleshing, thrusting
it deep in the earth, shaking it to and fro till the earth
was riven and widened, till the rivers ran down in the
rift where no man could find them.   Then in the ruined
land Hí-nu-no laughed and lay down in the shade of
his arrows.   Saying: This is a matter my brother will
not soon have mended.

When it was told Pa-ma-quásh of the anger dance of his
brother; how the hills had been scooped and strewn and
the rivers made to run in a rift deeper than man would

adventure to find them, Pa-ma-quásh lighted his medicine pipe and sat smoking. Out of the smoke of his pipe a cloud took shape, it arose, it floated over the land. Pa-ma-quásh arose with it, in the shape of a cloud he arose, he floated. He saw how his brother had trampled the land like a stag in his mating wrath, how the earth had been rived by the knife of Hí-nu-no and the rivers sunk, and his heart was wroth with his brother.

Thus it is said by our fathers, that Pa-ma-quásh, from his cloud discovered his brother, in the midst of the ruined land, asleep in the shade of his arrows. For there was no tree left, nor large rock for shelter. Into the sand Hí-nu-no had stuck his medicine arrows and lay with his head in the shade of their feathered shafts, and drunken with wrath, slept heavily. Then it was Pa-ma-quásh took away the medicine arrows from Hí-nu-no his younger brother, and with the cords of the sun he bound him.

Then said Pa-ma-quásh, By the cords of the sun I have bound you, I have taken your medicine arrows in which your power was, and you can do nothing against me. Here in this land you shall live, and the land shall remain as you made it. As for the rift of your knife, that shall be left as a memorial to your anger. And men seeing the gleam of the flint far down in the rift you have made, the name of that rift shall be Flint-Gash * forever.

But Pa-ma-quásh, because of the people, that the people might be fed, changed Hí-nu-no to the piñon pine tree.

* Colorado River and Canyon.

There in that land he abides and his brother visits him, Pa-ma-quásh who is the wind and the cloud and the rain, the remaker and mender.   Thus it is said by our Fathers.   Also it is a saying that he who goes into the country should be able to sleep in the shade of his arrows.   Thus said our Fathers' Fathers.

KATO CREATION MYTH [25]

A FRAGMENT

Collected by and translated with the help of
PLINY EARL GODDARD

The two Surpassing Beings of the Kato, having decided to destroy the first world and recreate a new, first build a new and higher sky to take the place of the one about to be destroyed, having four portals, four supporting columns, the north and south portals for the sun trails, the eastern portal for the clouds, and one in the west for the fog.   They then proceed to bring about the destroying Flood.

It was evening, they say,
The world was darkened with rain, they say;
It rained every day.
What is about to happen, the people said,
It rains every day!

Close to the ground the fog spread,
The sky was covered with clouds,
The people had no fire then,
The fires dwindled, they went out altogether;
All the creeks were full,
There was water in the valleys;
The waters encompassed the land.

The Flood is made; I have finished; said the Thunder.
It is made: said Nagaitcho, Let us ascend.

147

We will ascend to the upper sky, said Nagaitcho,
To the new sky that we have made.
At night, when all is asleep,
To the four-wayed heaven
We will ascend, they said.

Thus when the people slept, the Flood came, they say.
The waters came together everywhere,
There was no dry land left, nor mountains,
Nor were there any rocks standing above the waters,
Trees and grass were not, they say,
Nor any growing things.
Deer were not, nor the round-horned elk,
Grizzlies were not, nor pumas,
Wolves were not, they say,
Nor the small black bears of the brush country.
All these were washed away.
All the fourfooted kind,
Foxes, and grey squirrels, sharp nosed mice, even,
They were washed away.
There were neither ravens nor owls,
Nor orioles nor mocking birds;
The blue heron and the sand-hill crane,
They were all washed away,
The linnets and the meadow-larks,
The waters washed them away.

In the original, the list of animals and birds is indefinitely
extended to include all the species known to the recitor.
When the list is exhausted, the narrative goes on as follows:

Then the wind was not, they say,
When the waters were over the land,
There was neither frost nor snow;
Neither was there rain, they say,
Nor did it thunder,
When no trees were, to bring the thunder down;
Nor did the lightning appear.
Then clouds were not in the vault,
Nor fog out of the west-way.
Then the stars were not, but dark was;
Darkness, they say, enveloped the waters.

When the waters were over the land,
Then the sun walked not the sky-roads;
The way thereof was utterly dark.
Then the Earth-animal got up in the north,
The surpassing earth-creature
With its long horns, got up;
It walked this way through the deep places,
The water rose to its shoulders.
When it came to the shallows it looked up;
Its horn emerged from the waters;
There is a great ridge there, they say,
Upon which the waters break ceaselessly.
When it came to the middle place, in the east
The earth-animal looked up under the place of the sun-rise;
There is a great land there, they say,
Toward the sky-gate
Where the earth looked up.

Far away to the south it looked up,
It walked under the world surface;

Coming from the north, it walked southward;
There it lay down.
On the earth's head Nagaitcho was carried,
Standing upright, on the earth's head,
To the south he was carried.
Where it lay down, the earth-animal,
Its head he placed as it should be;
Between its eyes grey earth he placed, they say.
With reeds and clay he built up land,
He caused grass and green herbs to stand upright.
The head of earth-animal was buried out of sight.
On each of its horns Nagaitcho spread soil,
The small rocks he piled around them.
Let them be mountains here, he said;
And mountains became.

I am the land maker, said Nagaitcho,
I will go north, he said,
I will go around the land that I have made,
I shall fix it, he said, I shall finish the land.

As he went, he placed mountains about,
He caused the land to stand up against the waters.
Redwoods and pines he placed along the shore,
The fir and the spruce also.
At the tail of the earth in the north
He caused the fir and the spruce to grow;
As he went he looked back and saw them growing.
From the north he put down great rocks,
Over there the ocean beats against them.
He set mountains round about;

This he did continuing toward the south.
He dragged out creek beds with his foot
For the waters to run back off the earth;
He kicked out springs in the hills.
This he said, will be water for drinking.
All creatures shall drink of it; it shall not be salt.
Of the salty places he said, these will be deer licks.
Where valleys were required for streams to run in,
He set the land on edge.
As he worked with them, the mountains grew,
As he looked behind him Nagaitcho saw them growing;
The redwoods grew very tall.

Let acorns grow he said, and tan bark oak.
There will be brush on this mountain, he said,
Here many Grizzlies were living.
He made manzanita and white thorn grow there.
This shall be a valley he said,
Where deer shall be in great numbers.
White pines and black oaks he stood up,
When he looked back he saw that they had grown,
The mountains loomed up.
He tasted the springs that he had made,
He saw that the water was good.
His dog was with him as he went about the earth,
Drink, my dog, said Nagaitcho,
He himself drank of the water he had made;
Thus it shall be for animals and birds to drink of.
Walk behind me, my dog, said Nagaitcho;
Thus they went about the earth firming it.

He put rocks along the banks of the streams,
White stones he placed along them.
This shall be a small stream, he said,
Minnows and trout shall abound in it.
In this creek there shall be eels living,
Hook-bill and black salmon shall run up in this creek,
Last of all steel-head shall swim up it.

He put down yellow pines and redwoods in one place,
He set small black bears there,
Here the water shall be black,
It shall not be for drinking,
Here owls shall frequent, the screech and the elf-owl.
There shall be sparrow hawks about.

    The list continues until the earth is furnished with all varieties of birds and animals.

How will the ocean behave? said Thunder.
The water will rise up in ridges, said Nagaitcho,
It will settle back again,
There will be sand along the water,
On top the sand will glisten;
Old kelp will come ashore,
Old whales will wash ashore there,
Many kinds of fish shall live there,
The people will eat them.

    After finishing the new earth, Nagaitcho turns north again.

Walk behind me my dog, he said,
We will look at that which has taken place.
Walk fast, my dog, he said;
They drank of the water that had become,
They saw that it was good.
The valleys had broadened,
The streams were flowing,
Between the trees the brush was growing;
I have made a good earth, my dog, he said.
Acorns grew on the oaks, hazelnuts ripened,
The berries of manzanita were whitening,
Many deer fed in the meadows.
All things had grown and matured.
We have made them good, my dog,
The mountains have grown up quickly.
The air is warm, my dog,
It is pleasant to live in.

He turned his steps to the north, away from the earth head,
We will go back, my dog,
Look how the mountains have grown!
We are about to arrive, he said,
We are close home, my dog,
I am about to arrive in the north,
I am about to get back to my home in the north.
He said to himself three times,
I am about to arrive,
It is finished.

THE SAYINGS OF THE ANCIENT MEN [26]

SELECTIONS FROM THE TRIBAL RITES OF THE OSAGE

Collected by FRANCIS LA FLESCHE

From the Initiation of the Chief Rites of the Honga; the second movement of the ritual of the Black Bear.

Verily, at that time and place, it is said, in this house:

The sacred ceremonial house of the Honga, a people of seven fireplaces, seven war circles, who have taken the white throated black bear to be their life symbol:

When the moon of the mating of deer was still young, the Black Bear who is without blemish, was seized with a sudden desire of hibernation; being beset and perplexed with such strong desiring to and fro she ran to each of the four world quarters, returning again and again to the place of starting; after a time she paused, she stood, she considered, then swiftly she went, with hurried footsteps and came to the place of the bunch grass.

Verily at that time and place, it is said,

She gathered the tufts of grass compactly together, gathered them toward herself and laid them under her haunches, but no rest for her body she found.

In the same manner and words the bear is described as approaching the scrub oak, the red bud tree, the grapevine, the scattered stones, finding no rest thereon.

154

Verily in that time and place, it is said,

She went forth with hurried footsteps, reaching the rocky brow of a cliff whereon there were many stones which she arranged around her till the shape of a house was made, wherein entering, a flat cap stone, over her head she placed, as it were the roof of a dwelling.   Between the walls she had made, the sacred Black Bear sat down on her haunches and rested.

In that time and place, verily it is said

Nigh unto seven moons, the Black Bear rested.

Verily in that time and place, it is said

Inwardly thought as she sat; even now I have reached the end of the great division of days, the days of my hibernation, the beginning and end of seasons.

Truly in every direction around her she heard the voices of birds, calling to one another, heard as she sat in her house, the birds singing to one another for the change of seasons.

Again she inwardly thought; even now I have reached the end of division of days.   Swarms of insects she saw as she sat in her house, swiftly flying hither and yon in the air. And she thought in her heart, I have reached the season of birth, the days of the bringing forth.

Verily at that time and place, in this house it is said,

The Black Bear thought to herself behold I have come to Wakónda,[27]

I have arrived and am entering into the season of birth. Thus she thought of herself as she sat.   Verily, these my children must dwell in the four divisions of days: infancy, youth, adulthood, old age.

So she gathered her young in her arms and to the great god of the day, newly risen, she lifted her children,

And she said, O Ancient of Days, O Venerable Father, these my little ones have now become persons; give them strength, as they travel the path of life, that they attain to old age, O Venerable Father!

Verily, thus she said.

> *Kinon Wigie, recited by the priest for the face painting of the Initiates.*

Verily, at that time and place, in this house, it is said,

They the people of the seven fireplaces, said: the children have nothing with which to paint their faces.

Then he, the priest who personates the Black Bear, made answer:

When the children of the Black Bear paint their faces They shall use as a symbol the first-appearing, opener of day, the god who strikes the heavens with red; the color of that god they shall put upon their faces.   Thus they shall attain to old age, the path of life pursuing.

Verily at that time and place, it is said,

By the Black Bear on whom no fault lies, by that animal also

The children shall cause themselves to be known to Wa-kónda When they paint their bodies with charcoal, when they make themselves to be the color of the sacred, white throated Black Bear travelling the path of life they shall be identified by Wakónda.

Behold said the Black Bear,

The white spot on my throat; behold the god who sitteth in the midst of the day.

They shall press close to the god, it is said, placing that spot as his symbol, the white spot of the Sun, they shall make him to be in them; thus they shall attain to old age the path of life pursuing.

Song of the Priest who Impersonates the Black Bear, as he rises from the Initiation

Recitative

O my younger brothers!
I am about to rise,
Younger Brothers!
As the Black Bear on whom no blemish lies!
Truly in his likeness I shall rise,
O, younger brothers!
Thus the tribesmen who made of him their life symbol
Shall always see old age as they travel the path of life.
I am about to rise
My younger brothers!

Song

To the house that stands yonder
To the house that stands yonder
To the house that stands yonder

I go forth.
To the house where dwell the great black bears,
The Holy ones,
To the house that stands yonder, I go forth.

Recitative
My grandfather is the great Black Bear,
The Black Bear that is without blemish,
Of power amazing, O younger brothers.
When the Wa-zhá-zhe and the Tsí-shu
Make use of his strong magic
They shall always have the means to reach old age.

> *Selections from The Chief's Vigil wherein the various*
> *animals give their powers to the gens that adopt them as*
> *Life Symbols*

Verily at that time, at that place, it has been said, in this
house, the Wa-zhá-zhe, a people possessing seven fireplaces, were gathered together.
One of the Wa-zhá-zhe, of the Ponka gens, fell into deep
meditation upon his future course.
Verily at the end of the lodge he sat, where he fell pros-
trate, where he lay with his head bowed low.   Verily at
that time, at that place, it has been said in this house
He took that which the people have sanctified, he took
the soil of the earth and laid it upon his forehead.
And at the day breaking cried without ceasing, as he
wandered, walking forthwith toward the unfrequented
places.
Truly then he arrived at edge of the village where he sat
down, where he rested, while the great god of the day ar-

rived at mid-heavens and the darkness of evening came upon him,

Verily, in the midst of the prairie where trees grow not, he inclined his head to the right, he sat to rest on the earth, with his body bent low, and Wakónda made his eyes to close in sleep.

Verily, at that time and that place, it has been said, he woke and thought, the light of the god of day is spreading over me.

Then he took of the sacred earth and put it upon his forehead, and at daybreak he cried without ceasing, even as he went forth to wander to the unfrequented places, as he sat to rest on the earth and the day-god reached to mid-heaven,

As the darkness of evening came upon him, yet he ceased not his cry as he wandered in the midst of the open prairie where trees grow not.   As he sat upon the ground he thought, this spot also may be the dwelling place of Wakónda.

This he repeated for six days, and on the evening of the seventh he came to the head of a stream and stood close to it, and his vision was vouchsafed him.   In this vision the various animals which became the life symbols of the gens revealed themselves.

The Deer
Behold the young male deer whose horns are of dark grey. That one shall be a symbol to the children when they make of me their bodies, painting them like unto the colors of my body,

Said the male deer. Verily: they shall have power even as I have, to evade all danger,

When my enemies pursue me with arrows that fly around me in forked lines as they pursue and surround me and the herd, my companions, yet with the power of fleetness I can escape these dangers,

Verily it has been said at that time and place, when the children make of me their life symbol, they also shall have power to escape life's dangers.

The man of the Wa-zhá-zhe, of the Ponka gens who kept vigil, said:

Verily at that time and place, it has been said in this house, why should they make of the deer their symbol? It is for them, so that they should be able to make the quarry appear for the appeasing of hunger.

Under the branches of the white oak I have made a playing ground for the deer, under the branches of the red oak, where the ground is trodden soft by many hooves, Under the branches of the long acorn tree, under the twisted oaks I have made playing ground for the deer. When the dark acorn tree is approached by the knowing ones, the Initiate, in their hunting, there the deer shall not fail to appear.

Under the branches of the low, stunted oaks I have made a playing ground, I have not made it without purpose. All these I have made to be a snaring place, when the Initiate come to the snaring places the quarry shall not fail to appear.

Verily in that time and place, it has been said in this house, he said to them, he the Wa-zhá-zhe, called Ta-tha-xin, behold this Bunch grass which also is not made without a purpose.

When the Initiate approach the grass of the earth the quarry shall not fail to appear, even before the beginning of the day. And in the evening of the day the quarry shall not fail to appear.

When they of the Honga and they of the Tsí-zhu make of the deer their life symbol, the quarry shall not fail to appear.

The Beaver

Behold the beaver; when the children make of it their symbol, they shall always live to see old age.

Seven willow saplings the beaver brought to the right side of his house, dragging them with his teeth, piling them together,

Then he spake, saying: I have made these saplings to represent the seven military honors, Verily I, as a person, have made them, that the Initiates should always be able to count their honors rightly.

Against the current of the river the beaver put forth, rippling the surface of the water as he pushed forward, saying, behold the forked parting of the waters behind me, when the children make of me their life symbol, the gods shall always make way for them as for me the waters.

He struck the surface of the water with his tail, making a cracking noise as he pushed forward, saying, these strokes I make, not without purpose.

Toward the setting of the sun are our enemies, in striking the waters I strike the enemies of our people. Thus it shall be with the children who make of me their life symbol.

The Rattlesnake

From the midst of the bunches of tall grass the great snake, the Rattler, caused itself to be heard with a sound of buzzing,

That snake also spake, saying: Even though the Initiate pass into the realm of spirits by clinging to me, by using my strength they shall recover their consciousness, they shall be alive again in the realm of spirits.

The great snake, making a sound like the blowing of wind, close to the feet of the sick as he stood, repeatedly sounded his rattle.

Close by the head of the sick again and again, he sounded his rattle.   Toward the east wind, toward the west wind, toward the wind from the cedars he sounded his rattle,

Then the great snake spake, saying:

Even though the children pass into the realm of spirits, by my aid they shall always bring themselves back to consciousness.

When they make of me their life symbol the four great divisions of days they shall reach successfully; into the days of peace and beauty they shall make their entrance.

The Bull Elk

Verily, it has been said . . .

Behold the male elk that lieth upon the earth.   Verily I am the person who makes the bull elk to draw from the yellow boulder its power.

Behold the Watse-Miga, the woman-star of evening, Verily I am the person who maketh the yellow boulder to draw from the evening star its power.

When the Initiate make of me their life symbol even the

gods themselves shall stumble over them and fall.

Even the gods themselves as they move over the earth, pass around me as I sit immovable as the yellow boulder. Even the gods themselves fear to set teeth in me in anger. When the knowing ones make of me their bodies, the gods themselves shall pass around them, they shall fear to set teeth upon them in anger.

Verily, at that time and place, it has been said, the bull elk said to them: Even the gods fear to stare me in the face with insolence.

I am difficult to overcome by death. When the Initiate make of me their bodies even the gods themselves shall fear to stare them in the face with insolence, even the gods shall find them difficult to overcome by death,

Verily, it has been said, they shall fear to set teeth upon them in anger. They who make of me their bodies shall always live to see old age, the four successive life stages they shall always reach and enter.

Peaceful Day

Verily at that time and place, it has been said the Tsí-zhu, a people who possesss even fireplaces, spake to a gens of the Tsí-zhu, called No-Anger.

Verily a people who made their abode in the calm and peaceful days, verily one who removed from the gods all signs of anger, verily one who stands as having no anger or violence.

And a man of the Tsí-zhu questioned saying, Grandfather, the little ones have nothing whereof to make their life symbol.

And the one who was called No-Anger replied, saying: I

am a person whose being abides in the moist, vibrating air of the earth. Peaceful Day is the personal name I have taken.

When the knowing ones make of me their life symbol, they as a people shall ever abide, as they travel the path of life, in the days that are calm and peaceful.

Of the Peace Pipe I have made my body: when the Initiate make of it their bodies, by making it their life symbol they shall live without anger or violence, they shall use it, the Peace Pipe, in seeking earthly riches, they shall enable themselves to find goods in abundance.

APPENDIX

Note 1. Robert MacDougall, New York University. *Psychol. Rev.*, 1903.

Note 2. "Rhythmical forms are not in themselves rhythms; they must initiate the factor of movement in order that the impression of rhythm shall arise. . . ."—MacDougall.

"La marche de l'energie."—Landry.

"We have every reason to consider the movements of locomotion as the natural origin of rhythmic perception. . . ."—Wundt.

"In the development of rhythm the motor activity of the skeletal muscles plays the most important rôle. . . ." —Swindle.

"My method (of teaching rhythm) is a matter of muscular experience. . . ."—Dalcroze.

"One may assume that in all cases of rhythm there is a cycle of movement sensation involved. . . ."—Stetson.

Note 3. I say nothing here of the difficulty of coördinating the rhythms presided over by the autonomic nervous system, with those of the intellect. No work has been done in this field, which warrants me in stating as a fact what I surmise to be the case, namely that the two are instinctively, but not always successfully coördinated—and in every case where I use the term "instinct," I refer to coördinations achieved as a result of habitual experiential adjustment to environment. Perhaps the intellectual centers have not lived in the same house with the autonomic centers long enough for this to take place with sureness in every emergency, but such coördinations must still, for the generality of men, be accomplished by directed effort.

The Greeks and the Amerinds are the only people who seem thoroughly to have understood this, though all primitive people, even as low in the scale as the Boto-Cudos, are seen fumbling at it. The Greeks had a highly wrought system for integrating the personality by rhythmic muscular reactions. Our own systems of education not only ignore the necessity for such integration, but are for the most part presided over by men whose intellectual rhythms are developed apart from, and sometimes at the expense of, the autonomic rhythms. The Amerind, however, attains a degree of personal orchestration which enables me to treat him as Whole Man.

NOTE 4. Dalcroze, who deals with rhythm as we have to deal with it here, as a mode of expression, says unhesitatingly, "Yes, surely, rhythm is inherited." But an inheritance of this nature does not pass intact like the family jewels from parent to offspring. It passes by way of the capacity of germ plasm for subtle and continuing adaptations to the environment, in the cumulative disposition to respond to stimuli that remain constant in the environment. It appreciates from generation to generation in proportion to the release of old habits and inhibitions, as a response to streams of rhythmic impressions arising in new concepts of the environment. Probably it passes more easily in the completed circuit of the communal mind, and sparks only intermittently to conscious experiential contacts.

NOTE 5. Try rearranging some of the passages in which Dickens let himself go emotionally, such as the death of Little Nell, so that it resembles a modern free verse poem, and you will discover that that is precisely what it is. Any number of similar instances can be found in the works of Hardy and Meredith, as John Livingston Lowes has already pointed out, taken at the very crest of creative perception, fifty years in advance of our recognition of them as rhythms of poetic evocation.

NOTE 6. I shall probably not wait much longer. Before we can have any account of group-mindedness which can be built into our theories of art and society, somebody must make a long cast at the nature of mind as phenomenon. Is the human organism—any organism—a trap to catch mind-stuff, catching as high a voltage as the mechanism can hold? Or is the mind an entity taking up its residence in the organism and employing it on the business of its own adumbration? How can we have any real understanding of group-mindedness until we measure the units of which a group-mind is made? Has the mind a skin, a surface integument which marks the point at which my mind ends and yours begins, and is the contact in states of swarm and flock and mob, one of surface tensions? Or is mob-mindedness a common state of alikeness, produced by throwing a number of distinct individual minds into the same rhythmic mode? Take the simple phenomenon of a man running mob-mindedly to a lynching, who stubs his toe and finds himself suddenly sprawling on the ground utterly deprived of his mob impulse. This might be because he had been jolted out of the mob rhythm, or because, his energization being suddenly withdrawn from his surface contacts to consider the case of his toe, those contacts instantly ceased.

Every now and then I am stopped in my thinking about art and society because nobody can tell me these things. I find it immensely important to this study of rhythm to know whether there was, in the beginning, any such thing as an individual mind as we know it now; whether, in fact, there was anything but a delicate web of consciousness, sustained from point to point of individual existence. There are times when I seem to discover in the universal primitive belief in the distribution of mana, orenda, wakonda, god-stuff, elan vital, throughout animate nature, a subconscious memory of the web, and the slight differentiation between such points of contact as a bear and a man. Did man then become the capitalist of mind-stuff? And when a Paiute or a Boto-Cudo tells you that he does not know what he thinks until he has talked with other members of the tribe, does this mean that he cannot think with the little mind which he calls his own, but must resort to the pooled cognition of the group?

Is the original web still there, so that when members of the civilized group cease to communicate with words, they have no resort but to drop back, far back into the Dawn period for contact by means of the primitive wakonda? And is this why mob action is always so far below the plane of achieved intelligence?

Somebody, I say, must make a clean guess at these

things before we can prove whether they are true, and since the function of Science is to undertake vicariously for Society the supreme abnegation of all guessing, it might as well be I as anybody who makes the first throw. Personally I don't mind admitting that I have netted nothing but the air, and in any case I can probably get away with it by calling it poetry.

NOTE 7. There is, of course, always the contingency in refuting anything that Freud has said, that any day one may be confronted with an entirely new explanation of what Freud meant when he said it. But in any case, I know nothing of the Dawn Man which can be covered with a blanket term like "libido," and I do know enough of the earlier phases of human consciousness to deny that even Neolithic man can be adequately described in the phraseology of the neurological clinic. Freud's attempt to do so in "Totemism and Taboo" is about as successful in accounting for those elements in primitive life as the Marxian doctrine of economic determinism counts for the human infant's willingness to eat anything once.

NOTE 8. See *The Flock,* and *Love-and-the-Soul-Maker* (Austin)

NOTE 9. As we use the term jazz, it implies a particular kind of musical rhythm which requires the body to respond to it by particular, and unusual, movements. Actually jazz is a group of movements which have become exteriorized in musical intervals and accents. The movements are probably the Dawn Man's muscular record of the path of certain emotional—that is to say, chemical—alterations of his primary self, the autonomic self. I have already explained that the Dawn Man was probably much more responsive to these interior adjustments than we are, as his awareness of them was more acute.

Jazz is a reversion to almost the earliest type of response of which we are capable. That would imply a certain amount of disintegration of later and higher responses, which would make an excessive, exclusive indulgence in jazz as dangerous as the moralists think it. At the same time an intelligent use of jazz might play an important part in that unharnessing of traditional inhibitions of response, indispensable to the formation of a democratic society out of such diverse human materials as America has to work with.

NOTE 10. This of course would be the case if I am correct in supposing the major state of the primitive mind to be one of uncomplicated awareness. The capacity for shutting out or subordinating the rest of the stream of impressions for the purpose of concentrating on one impression, or one group of impressions, is acquired with difficulty. Our modern perception of a succession of sights or sounds as simple, means only that we have reduced it to simplicity by an act of volition, refusing to take into account any but the items concentrated upon.

Probably in the reproduction of rhythmic impression, selection is forced by the limitation of the number of rhythmic series which can be reproduced by a man's own body and its attached instruments. Further reduction may be forced by the necessity of standardizing the construction for concerted production.

NOTE 11. In this connection we recall that the Greek word for labor is from the same root as orgy, and that this term originally applied only to ecstatic states entered into by rhythmic movement. The same root word relation is found among many Amerind tribes, and the ritualistic refrain of many of their prayer dances is not, Lord have Mercy on us, but Work with us, work with us!

NOTE 12. I refer to the publication in my introduction to Mr. Cronyn's anthology of the poem called The Marriage Song of Tiakens without the note of my sources which were included in the introduction as originally written.

My first acquaintance with the marriage song was in some book of early travel in the Mississippi valley, where I found several lines of it quoted, but as at that time I had no idea that my studies would ever have any value to any one but myself, I copied the lines without making note of the source. Later when I came upon the whole song in Brinton, I accepted it as one does accept everything else that Brinton says about Amerind literature.

In making use of the Marriage Song to illustrate the likeness of Amerindian to Greek forms, I quoted Brinton as my source, not having seen at that time his final conclusion that the Taensa papers were forgeries, conclusions not reached by him for some years after his first acceptance of them as authentic. But the original introduction knocked about the publisher's office for two years, during which a portion of it was lost, as well as a more considerable portion of my interest in it, so that when publication finally occurred I had forgotten most of the details and never found it sufficiently important to refer to again.

What I think now is that the Marriage Song was a genuine fragment which Patisot discovered probably in the very traveler's record in which I first came across it. Possibly it was this fragment which gave him the idea for the whole forgery. However, there seem so many things more important to do than reopen this ancient discussion that I have never taken the trouble to confirm my own guess in the matter. The net result of the incident has been to make me extremely careful of accepting decisions of even the most outstanding ethnologists when they touch upon literary matters.

NOTE 13. The same practice of unpatterned musical accompaniment is reported by Miss Dinsmore as among the "White Indians" of the Central American *Tules*. It is also found in New Mexico among Los Hermanos Penitentes, performed on the flute in connection with their flagellations, and in a mixed Indian-Spanish ritual ballet called *Matichina*.

NOTE 14. Possibly I do the ape family an injustice. I have never had any apes to experiment upon. Nor have I any wolves or elephants, but rely on reports of other investigators. I have, however, been able to tell stories to sheepdogs and to trained hunting dogs, since these both are acquainted with explicit vocabularies by which the wishes of their masters are conveyed. In the case of the sheep-dog the vocabulary consists largely of arm signs operated at a flock length, but is none the less effective. I have also been able, in two or three instances, to communicate a sequence of activities to children of eight months, largely by associated sounds rather than by articulate words. Perhaps

when the kitten plays with a spool or a catnip mouse he
also is anticipating man in the invention of symbolic story.

Note 15.   This Creation Myth is of such majestic proportions
that in lieu of all comment I quote the following from Mr.
Cushing's translation:

[After the people issue from the underworld the Beloved Twins
firm the earth and make it fit for the first settlement of men.
Instructed by the Sun-father the elder says to the younger:]

That the earth be made safer for men, and more stable,
Let us shelter the land where our children be resting;
Yea! the depths and the valleys beyond shall be sheltered
By the shade of our cloud-shield! Let us lay to its circle
Our firebolts of thunder, aimed to all the four regions,
Then smite with our arrows of lightning from under.
Lo! the earth shall heave upward and downward with thunder!
Lo! fire shall belch outward and burn the world over,
And floods of hot water shall seethe swift before it!
Lo! smoke of earth-stenches shall blacken the daylight
And deaden the senses of them else escaping
And lessen the number of fierce preying monsters!
That the earth be made safer for men, and more stable.

[After the firming of the earth and the gift of corn through the
coming of the corn maidens the people are advised:]

It is well, brothers younger!
Dwell in peace by our firesides.
Guard the seed of our maidens
Each kind as ye see it,
Apart from the others.
And by lovingly toiling,
As by toiling and loving,
Men win the full favor
And hearts of their maidens,
So, from year unto year
Shall ye win by your watching,
And power of beseeching,
And care for the corn-flesh,
The favor and plenish
Of our seven Corn maidens.
They shall dance for the increase
And strength of the corn-seed,
Of each grain, making many —
Each grain that ye nourish
With new soil and water!

[The ceremonials for establishing the Priesthood of the Bow are described:]

> Soft they chanted the sacred song-measure,
> The magic and dread Shómitâk'ya,
> And whispered the seven fell names!
> Then they painted the round mark of thunder
> And the wavering trail of the lightning
> Around the great drum, in the middle,
> And on the hooped drum-stick of thunder.
> And over the drum-head, with prayer-dust
> They marked out the cross of the quarters,
> As on the cloud-shield they had leveled
> Fire-bolts to the four earthly regions.
> The fathers in thought bowed their faces,
> And secretly prayed, in their hearts.
> The people who watched them, held breath,
> And covered their mouths with their robes.
> In dread of the powers of magic
> And in woe for the doom of their fathers.
> The gods, to the right and the left
> Took their stand by the side of the waters,
> As erst they had stood by the cloud-shield,
> Their weapons of magic between them,
> The plumes of the warriors placed duly
> In lines, to the eastward before them;
> The warriors made ready for travel,
> Apart from, but circling around them.
> Then the Twain gave the word of beginning!
> The master of words raised his song-staff,
> On his shoulder the plume-wand of man-folk;
> The drum-master lifted his sound-hoop,
> In its circle the symbol of thunder,
> On its handle, the red sign of lightning;
> Six times did they lift up in silence
> The song-staff and hoop of the drum,
> Then struck, with the might of their sinews.
>
> (Vol. 13. Report of Bureau American Ethnology.)

NOTE 16. I had the original of this from a Sioux boy who was uncertain of its origin. Song-borrowing is frequent.

NOTE 17. Among tribes that have no fixed places of residence, the abandoning of old people, too feeble to travel, is usual. This is the only suggestion of protest that I have encountered; the plaint of the aged of all lands that death should ensue just when wisdom is attained. Miss Dinsmore records a similar woman song among the Pima.

NOTE 18.   The personal song is an expression of a man's own philosophy, or a note of his consummate spiritual experience.   It is often sung going into battle, or on the approach of death, in which case friends of the singer will often gather around his bed and sing it for him.

NOTE 19.   Songs of mystical seeking are found among all tribes.   This is probably the original of the one which Frank Burton translated as a sentimental love song.

NOTE 20.   This song sequence belongs to an ancient rain-provoking rite recently revived.   The first song appeared to have a number of archaic words, which renders the translation uncertain.   In many of the Pueblo songs one encounters repetitions of phrases and figures, occurring with the frequency of Homer's "wine-dark sea."

NOTE 21.   The occurrence of two nearly identical song motives in tribes widely separated is the evidence of the unity of tribal thinking.   The Piaute song is highly mimetic, unintelligible without its accompanying dance.

NOTE 22.   The Osage song is from an initiation rite recorded by Francis La Flesche, and is condensed merely to show the verse progressions controlled by ritual acts.

NOTE 23.   The Passamaquoddy, of whom a few isolated members are still to be found in the remote parts of Maine, were distinguished for the more than ordinary poetic content of their songs.   This example was collected last summer by Mary Wheelwright, and translated by the singer..

NOTE 24.   All four formulas were collected and literally translated by James Mooney, but it was not until I had additional material which I thought would bring out their poetic values that I ventured to restate them, with the help of Leota Harris, a woman of Cherokee descent, who had the formulas almost in the original form from her mother.   Even as rewritten the verses have too little of the hypnotizing murmur native to the language in which they originated.   Easily noticeable is the form of "affirmation" recently incorporated in the modern use of suggestion.   It is also worth remarking that the formula for turning aside a storm, in which the Wisher appears least, and the Wish is stressed, is most poetic in concept.

NOTE 25.   The Kato are located in California, not far from the Pomo group.   Their culture is in many ways more primitive than the Osage, and more completely disintegrated. This version of their creation myth was built up, with Mr. Goddard's aid, from two fragments secured by him and one collected by the author.

NOTE 26. These fragmentary excerpts from the Sayings have been abbreviated by reducing the number of ritual tags to avoid tediousness. The poetic values of these sayings are undoubtedly higher in the originals than in the present version, but I have refrained from attempting to carry them further until I can have careful and extensive hearings of the original language, in order to reëxpress, in so far as it can be done, the native sound patterns, the assonances and syllabic rhythms. Fearing that this will never be achieved, I publish what I have for the sake of the light it will throw on an unsolved problem. Here, perhaps, is the occasion to record what Mr. La Flesche once said in reference to the general exposition of Indian rhythm as it was expressed in the first edition. At a meeting of the Southwestern division of the Association for the Advancement of Science, I had just concluded a talk in which all that is written above had been briefly said, and the program was about to continue, when Mr. La Flesche asked permission as an Indian, to comment on my remarks. What he said was that something he had always known and often puzzled about, had been for the first time made intellectually clear to him. Not only did he agree with my rendering of Indian rhythm, but he adduced an interesting instance of the recitation of tribal lays, which, in eleven divisions, were given in recitative simultaneously, and yet produced an harmonious effect. I doubt if any such rhythmic orchestration of spoken verse is possible among moderns, even as duet, to say nothing of eleven voices.

NOTE 27. Wakónda is not personalized when used as in this instance, but signifies the individual encounter with Spirit, manifest in the birth of her young. Further on in the lay, where the man of the Ponka gens is wandering in search of a vision, he expresses the same idea of spiritual encounter saying: "This spot also may be the dwelling place of Wakónda."